LIFE ROCKS!

Tori Allen

TADA INK
Indianapolis, Indiana

LCCN: 2003109242

Proofread by Kim Heusel and Andrea Priest
Cover designed by Phil Velikan
Interior photography provided by Tori Allen
Front cover photos by Greg Epperson
Back cover photos by ESPN/Shazaam/Tony Donaldson

Printed in the United States of America
10 9 8 7 6 5 4 3 2 1

Published in the United States by Tada Ink., P.O. Box 502568, Indianapolis, Indiana, 46250. (317) 523-7625

This book is dedicated to Mrs. Guthrie and Mrs. Moore at Lawrence Central High School. Their freshman interdisciplinary class of Modern World Literature and Modern World Studies was the inspiration for this project. I will forever be indebted to them for their willingness to think "outside the box" in order to help a lost, formerly homeschooled, 13-year-old with dyslexia bloom into a capable student. All students should be able to learn history and literature (or any other subject for that matter) in such a hands-on, exciting and individualized manner. Most other teachers and their methods pale next to these two women. THANK YOU!!!!

Table of Contents

Life Rocks!

Part Three: School Rocks!

Meet the Real Tori Allen

Now this is the life! Me lounging on the beach in Mombasa, Kenya, at age seven.

Name: Victoria Ann Allen

Nicknames: Tori, "T", Toto, Tinky, Torbor

Birthdate: July 30, 1988

Height: 5'4"

Weight: 110 pounds

Favorite Foods: marshmallows and pecan pie

Favorite colors: pink and turquoise

Favorite animal: monkey

Favorite movie: *Princess Diaries*

Favorite book: *All-American Girl* by Meg Cabot

Favorite subject: math

Favorite sports: climbing and pole vaulting

Favorite hobby: kayaking

Life Rocks!

Favorite number: 72

Favorite cartoon character: Curious George

Pets: Two huge dogs named Shadrach and Mishach, one tiny black cat named Pippi

Dream job: lawyer, spy or kindergarten teacher

Dream place to live: Mombasa, Kenya, on the beach

Dream family: married with twin girls

Thing I am worst at: golf (it took me 173 strokes — not counting whiffs — and three hours, to golf seven holes last year)

Annoying thing I do: touch all ledges, corners, furniture as if they were climbing holds.

Thing that annoys me: when someone says something under his or her breath and then says, "oh, never mind."

Thing I sleep with: my stuffed monkey named Gorgie (I bought him with my own money the first time I competed in the Gorge Games.)

What I eat before I compete: pasta or rice the night before

My religion: Christian

Something I wish I could do: surf really well

Someone I wish I could meet: Mary-Kate and Ashley Olsen

Favorite Quote: "Perseverance means that you can't let go and still win."

Part One:
AFRICA ROCKS!

*Me (age five) sifting stones out of sesame seeds with
my African grandmother*

Clark and me (ages one and three)
playing in the park in Annecy, France

MY JOURNEY
FROM AUBURN TO AFRICA

Hi, my name is Tori Allen, and I am just like you. Really! This book is about my life and how I have enjoyed living every minute of it. I hope you love living your life as well, but if not, keep reading. You can have a life that rocks, too. It's all in your attitude and your actions. So don't just sit there, get started! We are off on an adventure together.

I'll start at the beginning. I was born in Auburn, Alabama, while my parents were college students at Auburn University. They loved it there so much that they almost named me Auburn. I lived in a tiny apartment with my parents and pet dalmation, Paco. When I was six months old we moved to Atlanta and began the period of my life that I call the nomadic years. During these seven years we moved 14 times. These moves took us to Atlanta, Georgia (twice); Fullerton, California; Pasadena, California; Albertville, France; Cotonou, Benin (in West Africa); Savalou, Benin; and Indianapolis, Indiana, just to name a few of the more memorable places. By the time I landed in Indianapolis at the age of nine, my passport was so full of entry and exit visas that the embassy had to add pages to it.

My three favorite places where I have lived are Atlanta, Georgia; Albertville France; and Savalou, Benin. I lived in

Life Rocks!

Atlanta two different times. The best part about both of these times was living with my grandparents. They built an entire apartment in their basement for our family. It had two bedrooms, a bathroom with a big bathtub, kitchen, fireplace, and a back door that walked out to a wooded yard and lake. I remember waking up early and going upstairs to eat lucky charms while Grandpa watched the news and drank his coffee. Almost everyday, my grandma would let me help her do dishes or clean. She let me make messes, but she still told me what a big helper I was. She had a huge bathtub with whirlpool jets in it. I loved to get in there, slide down the end, and put in tons of bubbles so that the jets would make a bubble mountain. To this day, I am very close to my Nana because of all the time we spent together.

I moved to Albertville, France, when I was three years old. We lived in an upstairs apartment over an old farmhouse. No matter what window we looked out, we saw snow-topped mountains all year-round. I called our landlady French Grandmudder because she gave us candy (bon bons) and let us pick cherries from her trees. My parents had to go to French classes from 8 a.m. until 4 p.m. each day so I went to the local public preschool which is called a *maternelle*. Not one person in my class spoke English so I had to learn French really fast. I was in a class of 24 three-year-olds with one teacher and one part-time aid. After being in school fours hours each morning, I ate lunch with my parents in their school's dining hall and then went back to my school for nap and more learning in the afternoon. After school we walked into town to buy loaves of bread that were longer than I was tall, and fresh veggies at the farmer's market. While I lived there, the town of Albertville hosted the 1992 Winter Olympic Games. I saw U.S. hockey games, bobsled races, ski jumping, and figure skating. France was magical.

Even though I can find something good to say about every place I have lived, my favorite place in the world is Africa. I lived for one year in the port city of Cotonou in the West

African country of Benin. We lived there in order to get used to the new language called *Fon* and to make sure that we had all the information and supplies we needed to live and work in a small village. In Cotonou, I went to an African kindergarten. There were no walls around the rooms. Each class had a grass roof held up by poles. Under the roof we had tables, supplies in storage containers, and shelves. My school bus was the back of a moped. After that year, we moved to a village called Savalou. I loved Savalou and my friends there so much that I will always consider myself to be part African. If it had been up to me we would have never left my village. In the next few chapters I will tell you more about my daily life in Savalou.

What about you?

1. Think about the places you have lived. List them all.

_____   _____

_____   _____

_____   _____

2. List one or more special person and memory attached to each place.

_____   _____

_____   _____

_____   _____

Life Rocks!

Take Action!
Write a letter to one of your extended family members and one friend you have not seen in awhile and tell each about a special memory you have with them. Make sure to tell them why they are special to you.

Mom, Clark, and me (age five) by our swing set behind our house

MY AFRICAN HOUSE

From the time I was born until I was five we moved an average of once every seven months. Most of the time, I shared a room with my brother or both of us shared a room with our parents. When it came time to move to our house in the village of Savalou, we were really excited. We planned on living there for several years, and we each were getting our own room! We helped pack for the move with great anticipation.

The first problem was actually finding a house in the village. Most were either being lived in or were crumbling down. In the end, my parents rented a house for $15 a month. It was the future retirement home of a man who lived in the capital city. We offered to rent it from him and fix it up. It was at the end of the paved road heading north, and at least it had sturdy walls and a roof that didn't leak very much.

We took several trips to the village from the capital city to fix up the house. It was a four-hour drive on pitted roads. My new house had a tin roof, cement floors, and wooden slats for windows. On our first trip up to the village, all we did was shovel bat poop out of the house and the ceiling. It was really gross. The next time we were able to staple some screen over the windows and paint the walls. Once the doors were on, we moved in.

Life Rocks!

It was a big house to me. It had three bedrooms and a gathering room at the front. The front porch was covered so we could sit there and stay dry during rainy season. Since the house sat on a hill we had a great view of the end of the village from our porch. Away from the house was the cooking room, which we attached to the house by adding an eating porch between the kitchen and house. Then there were typical African storage rooms and our laundry area next to the house.

We had a large garden behind the house with corn (that got eaten by the rats), pineapple, yams, and salad. We even built a chicken coop, guinea pig cages, and rabbit hutches next to the garden. Along the side of the house banana plants and papaya trees grew like crazy. In the back yard, my dad used tree trunks and made a swing set that had a tire swing and a rope ladder. Our yard eventually had grass but when we first moved in, there was only gravel so we had to move that out before the grass could grow.

We had an indoor bathroom. There wasn't hot water, but since it was so hot outside, we didn't need it. We could always heat water on the gas stove and pour it in the bathtub if we wanted a hot bath. We had electricity from seven in the evening until midnight. That meant that we planned to do things like computer work in the evening. That also meant we had lights and fans for a few hours of relief!

My brother and I decided to share a room again so we could make the other room our playroom. In the play room, my dad built a loft for us with a railing around it that looked like a row of happy faces. To get up on the loft, we climbed a rope ladder. To get down, we had a slide. Underneath the loft were three rows of cubbies for our toys. We took all the doors off the bedrooms of the house so that the air could move around and it wouldn't be too stuffy.

Our furniture was made out of teak wood. We had tons of bookshelves but the dust was so bad that we had to put curtains on them. We also had to push the books to the backs of the shelves so that the mice couldn't build nests behind the books.

Since our table was on a covered porch between the house and kitchen, sometimes we got rained on, and other times, swarming bugs attacked us. The worst bugs were the flying termites. To top it off, the counter in the kitchen was about three feet high. That was perfect for me but killed my mom's back.

I loved that home because people always came to visit and eat with us. We also had many adventures with animal intruders. Once, a green mamba snake got in our bedroom. Another time, millions of army ants invaded our house and even killed our rabbits and chickens. Almost every night we heard rats scratching in the ceiling. Sometimes they would even run through the hall and the dogs would chase them out. The worst things, though, were the scorpions. They scared me.

Life was one big adventure in Savalou — kind of like camping out in my own house.

What about you?

1. How is your life like an adventure?

_____

_____

_____

2. What makes your house special to you?

_____

_____

_____

_____

Take Action!
Brainstorm ways to help people who do not have a house to come home to.

Georgie and me (age seven) all dressed up

MY MONA MONKEY

One dusty night during dry season, there was a knock at our gate. My mom shooed us into the house as she went to see who was there. When she opened the gate, a man entered carrying a sack. He kept trying to get my mom to look in the sack, but my mom wouldn't. It was pretty normal to have hunters and other villagers bring us animals to buy. We already had a tortoise named Trickey, a dikdik (a miniature deer), rabbits, chickens, guinea pigs, two dogs, a cat, and a hedge hog. The last thing my mom wanted was another baby animal to nurse. As they talked, I snuck out on to the porch to see what might be in the bag. I heard a small cry coming from the bag and then I heard the word "singe," which is French for monkey, and I went nuts. I started jumping up and down begging my mom to take it. She knew it was not worth saying no, so she paid $5 and Georgie was ours.

Georgie was just a few days old. She did not have fur or any color in her skin so we could not tell what kind of monkey she was until she was older and her coloring came in. She didn't have any teeth, either. Apparently, earlier that day the farmer saw a monkey in his fields and he shot her. He didn't want her messing up his crops, plus monkeys are hunted for food in Benin. When he went to retrieve the monkey, he lifted her and found a nursing baby hanging on her. He had heard that the foreigners might buy the baby animal so he brought it to us when he returned from the field. The challenge, then, was to keep Georgie alive. She had to be nursed with a baby bottle around the clock and kept very warm. She cried a lot if she wasn't being touched or held, and she couldn't move around on her own yet. We fed her concentrated baby formula and made a carrier out of cloth to keep her near us all day. After two weeks, she began to hop around a bit, and her teeth started to push through. She was saved!

As Georgie grew, so did the trouble she got into. We never tied her up during the day, but she slept in a large dog crate at night. She liked to curl up under the blankets. When she was in trouble, she would go to her crate, hide under the blankets, and rock back and forth. Georgie's favorite victim for her pranks was my dad. She would wait until he poured a glass of water and then she would go tip it over on his desk. Other times she would run through mud and then hop onto the laundry hanging on the line. Our clothes always had muddy monkey prints on them. She made such big messes by tipping things over that we tried to block her from getting in the house. Georgie got in anyway by riding on the back of the dog who would hit the screen door with her paw until it bounced open and she could stick her nose inside. As soon as the dog was in, Georgie would jump off and run and steal something like a puzzle piece or a cookie from the table. Then she would squeal and run to hide.

In addition to riding on the dog's back she did other things to bug the animals. When the cat, named Monkey, would walk through the family room, Georgie would hide under the couch and run out and grab her by the tail. Then Georgie would drag the cat around by her tail until she was bored with that game. Other times, when the German shepherd was sleeping Georgie would go up to him, pull open his eyelids and peek in, or pull up his lip and grab his tooth. The dog would just lay there until he was really tired of being bugged, and then he would snap at the monkey to warn her. Georgie would squeal, jump out of reach, and then do it again a few minutes later. Georgie had pouches in her cheeks so we would often find her digging in the medicine cabinet stuffing pink antibiotic tablets in her mouth as fast as possible. When we caught her we would have to push the antibiotics out of the pouches one by one. One time she had nine tablets in there at once.

Just a few months before we were supposed to return to the USA, we went on a three-week trip around West Africa. We left Georgie at home with some of our friends who stayed at our house and took care of all the animals. One night, after a terrible day in Ghana where our car was broken into and all our important papers including our passports and shot books were stolen, we called home and found out Georgie was dead. I guess a green mamba snake had snuck into her crate and, when she went to bed, she startled the snake and it bit her. I cried for the whole next week. Georgie, my mona monkey, was the best pet I have ever had.

What about you?

1. List all the pets you have ever had or ever wanted to have.

_____   _____

_____   _____

_____   _____

2. What are the funniest things a pet you know has ever done?

_____

_____

_____

_____

Life Rocks!

3. How are pets a good way to learn responsibility?

_____

_____

_____

_____

Take Action!

Go to an animal shelter and walk a few dogs and play with a few cats for several hours. If you enjoy it, find out information on volunteering at the shelter more often.

Clark and me (ages two and four) with Etienne the dog and Mermaid the cat in front of our felt Christmas tree at our first Christmas in Africa

MY MEMORIES
OF CHRISTMAS

Purim… Halloween… May Day… Thanksgiving. You name it, we celebrated it in Benin. Sometimes we celebrated a certain holiday as part of learning about a new culture. Mostly we celebrated various unusual holidays as a way to have fun and amuse ourselves while we tried to pass the long hot days. For Purim we'd dress up as bad guys and queens, read the story of Esther, and make three-cornered-hat cookies. We got this idea from a book on Jewish holidays. For Halloween, we'd dress up with our friends and parade around the house getting candy in a bag as we passed each adult. Thanksgiving was a challenge because we had to think about our turkey in the middle of summer. We would buy him and fatten him up in a cage until Thanksgiving eve when we would kill him. Of all the holidays, though, my favorite memories are from our Christmases in Benin.

Our first Christmas was really kind of sad. My grandparents and friends had all collected boxes of Christmas presents in July of that year and had mailed them to us in Benin. We waited and waited for the presents. That Christmas, we did not have a tree; instead, we had two pieces of felt cut in the shape of a tree and sewn together. This was hung over a broom and stuffed with clothes to have a shape. The ornaments were felt pieces that my brother and I cut out and decorated with glue and glitter and stuck on the tree with Velcro. We were sure the boxes were going to arrive any day. That year we thought they'd at least arrive by Christmas morning. They didn't, and that was the beginning of our new perspective on Christmas; we began to appreciate the little gifts like pencils and African baskets and books rather than expect to get all the expensive things on our lists. We waited months for the boxes and finally gave up on them. The boxes did eventually arrive, though, two years later. They were mildewy and ruined, and the things that were not ruined were clothes that we had outgrown and toys that were too childish for us by then.

After that, my brother and I vetoed the felt tree, and so we tried the African method of using a cotton plant as a Christmas tree. The puffs of cotton were like snow and the branches were long and spread out so we could hang things nicely. This was fun! We could paint the branches cheerful colors or wrap them in ribbons. We could even use glue and glitter to make the branches sparkle.

Once we got settled into the village of Savalou, we made lots of friends. I loved Christmas because we would buy special treats for our friends. Sometimes we would buy a family a large bag of rice and a new cooking pot. Or we would buy a young couple some pretty fabric to make matching Christmas outfits. All my friends would get coloring books and markers from America. About a week before Christmas, we would fill our wagon with gifts, and we would go around the village making deliveries like Santa. At every house we would stay and have a soda and a snack and talk to our friends about the news of the day, so the deliveries took many hours to finish.

Not many foreigners lived in Benin so we pretty much knew every foreigner and where each of them lived. My favorite non-African people were the Peace Corps volunteers. They were usually young, and they only stayed in Benin about two years. Our house was a gathering place for them, especially at Christmas. My mom always invited all the ones we knew to come to our house for holidays because she liked to cook them a nice meal and let them relax a bit. Every time we traveled she would pick up little gifts to put away until Christmas for any unexpected guests. She never wanted anyone to not have presents under the tree Christmas morning. On Christmas Eve, Mom and Dad would stay up all night wrapping gifts for the group of Peace Corps people who showed up. One year there were 18 people who came to Christmas at our house. Since it was hard to get wrapping paper, Mom would save barf bags from airplane trips and decorate them as gift bags. That year, we made cookies all day and set off fireworks at night.

The church in our village always had a big youth production on Christmas Eve. It was fun to go to even though it lasted about three hours. There were skits, songs, jokes, and food. When I was seven, I finally knew enough of the French and Fon languages to be in the program. I went to rehearsals three times per week for two months and really got to know the other kids. My brother did it, too. The night of the program he made everyone laugh the whole time because he had gotten cowboy boots for Christmas that year (hand-me-downs from a cousin in Iowa) and they were too big. All he did was stomp around and make funny faces rather than sing the songs we had practiced.

Christmas is not the same now. We never have unexpected guests. Mom doesn't collect gifts and barf bags. We don't even put up a tree because there is no one to share it with. I do miss all my friends from the village and I still try to send them fun gifts to open on Christmas. One day I want to really surprise them and show up in Savalou for Christmas pulling a wagon full of gifts!

Life Rocks!

What about you?

1. What are some of your favorite holiday memories and traditions?

_____

_____

_____

2. Find out the history behind each tradition. You may have to ask your grandparents or do some research.

_____

_____

_____

Take Action!

Start a book keeping track of the things your family does to celebrate special days.

Georgie the monkey "helping" me (age seven) do my math at Monkey Montain Academy

MY SCHOOL

Once we moved away from the city, my mom started homeschooling me. Our village did have a public school but there were 64 students in my class, with one instructor, no books, only enough desks for 40 students, and all the instruction took place in Fon, not French, so I was lost. Also, the teachers were on strike over 40 percent of the time, so even if I went to school my mom had to fill in for those missed days. Instead of stressing out trying to make sure I got enough instruction in English and enough time to go into the village and play, she decided to teach me herself. At first, she tried to teach me at the kitchen table each morning, but we never got anything done. You see, our house was busy with people visiting us all the time. People were curious about what we were doing so they would come in and pick up my crayons, color on my pages, do my math for me, try to read my books... it was useless. So, in order to make sure I got a good education, my dad built a small square building behind our house to be our schoolhouse. This way, when people came to visit my dad, they would not see us as easily and we could get things done quickly, without interruption.

Our school day lasted three hours a day, five days a week, 12 months per year. We took work with us on trips and used our travel days for field trips to zoos, rain forests, old forts, and historic sites. Both my brother and I were allowed to work at our own pace in each subject. That meant if we were good in a subject, like math, we could finish two years of work in one year. Yet, if we were having trouble in another subject we could slow down and make sure we understood the material completely before moving on. This was perfect for me because I have dyslexia. My mom figured this out after teaching me to read. Sometimes I would read things completely in reverse, and I never grew out of it like most kids do. I think being able to go at my own pace in reading and spelling, without knowing if I was "ahead" or "behind," enabled me to find ways to work around my reading challenge successfully. I never knew that I had a "problem," I just knew that I had to work harder at reading than at math.

Since we were the only English-speaking kids within a four-hour drive, my mom would often invite other English-speaking kids to visit us for a week or two each month and do school with us. She liked the fact that this gave us the feeling of a real classroom. Plus, she thought it would motivate us to see how our peers were doing in school. Katherine came most often. She lived four hours north, and she was from Australia. She was such a good writer that I could hardly wait for each of her visits, to hear the next part of the story she was writing. Kerri, an American, lived four hours to the south, and she came sometimes as well. Since she lived in the capital city, her visits were more for me than her. She was a hard worker so my mom liked having her in the class. I loved having these extra "sisters" every now and then.

I looked forward to having my mom to myself for those few hours each day. She read aloud to us, taught us about major works of art, helped us learn to identify the works of famous composers, played games with us, and patiently taught us all the subjects day after day. Some days it would rain so hard on the tin roof that I could not hear her voice when she read. On those days we did art projects instead. Other times, she would have us do two lessons in one day so that we could go into the village the next day and practice our Fon language skills. My favorite part was the math games. She taught us our math all the way up until third grade entirely through games. I think this is why my dyslexia did not affect my math skills. I learned math in my head and with my hands, not through numbers off a paper. I played with math until math was a part of me. I still love math.

Because we did school every day, all year-round, learning was a lifestyle. If we missed a school day we were bummed. School was often the place where our biggest adventures took place. Georgie, our monkey, always found a way to sneak into the school room. She would dump our craft boxes, bite erasers off the pencils, and pull things off the wall in order to eat the sticky tak. We had so many rats in the ceiling that sometimes we'd have to take a break and shoo them out so Dad could shoot them with the BB gun. One year, our dog had puppies, and the only safe place for them was in the school room so we did school with a litter of seven black pups tumbling around. Monkey Mountain Academy of Savalou, Benin, was the best school on earth.

What about you?

1. What are some things you have learned at home and not at school?

_____

_____

_____

_____

2. What are your favorite things to learn at school?

_____

_____

_____

_____

Life Rocks!

3. Think of your favorite teacher, what made him/her your favorite?

_____

_____

_____

_____

Take Action!

Draw a picture of your idea of a perfect school room. Include in the picture supplies, students, teachers, books, decorations, and subjects to be taught. Try to use your ideas to turn your room or playroom into a learning room for the summer. Invite your friends over to learn something new, be creative, and brush up for the next school year.

Clark and me (ages three and five) in front of traditional grain silos in our village.

MY VILLAGE

When you leave the swamplands of the coast and head north into Benin, the land stays flat for several hours. As soon as you see the first rock mounds, you turn west onto a worn out road. One hour down that winding, pitted road, you will see a ridge of hills. The road winds in front of the hills, and at the base of the hills is the village of Savalou spilling into the valley. Savalou is my village. It is a rather large village since it is the center of the "county." All the government offices for the area as well as a small hospital, area high school, and the major weekly market are in Savalou.

As sophisticated as all this sounds, Savalou is still very traditional. The first thing you will notice around the village are houses and high walls painted white with colorful murals. Usually the murals have writing in the Fon language mixed with pictures of mythical animals. These are voodoo coven houses. These houses hold secret societies for different voodoo groups. Throughout the year the women and men who belong to these groups go to the special houses to hold meetings with each other and the spirits they worship. These meetings last weeks at a time and involve days and days of drumming, dancing, and ceremonies with the members dressed in colorful costumes. Many times, the different societies in town get mad

23

at each other and spend days marching in front of each other's special meeting houses trying to disturb each other's meetings.

Another very traditional thing in my village is the king. When we first arrived in the village, the first person we had to officially greet was the king. When we went there, the king offered my dad one of his wives as a gift. It was very funny watching my dad politely refuse this gift. Even though there are a mayor and other official government people, the king still has a lot of political power over the happenings in the village. For example, one year the rains were very late in coming. The wells were muddy and almost dry, the cisterns were empty, and the reservoir was too low to be useful. It was a crisis. Well, it was the king who called together the Catholic priest, the voodoo societies, the pastors, and the village leaders and told them to all pray to their own gods and ancestors in order to bring the rain. The people respected him enough to obey immediately. That night, one group even danced in the streets without clothes on in a special ceremony for their god.

If you walk along the road that goes over a hilly pass between the ridges, you will go behind the hills and find the farmlands for the village. Right on the backside of the hill, before the land flattens out for the farms, is a group of women who break rocks. All day they sit under trees banging boulders with hammers breaking the large rocks into small stones or gravel that are used to make cement for building and brick making. This is their full-time job. The village farmers walk five to seven miles past these women each day to their fields. They plant ignams, manioc, and cotton. The first two are for food but the third is a crop that they grow to be sold to other nations for cash. Sometimes the farmers build little grass huts to sleep in when they are too tired to walk home.

At night the village stops working and becomes a social gathering. The people sit outside their homes with lanterns lit. People walk around visiting one another to catch up on the news of the day. The children play in the courtyards with balls. The old men play a game like mancala called quatre-quatre on benches under shelters. The young men play cards near the market where the light is good. The women cook over fires and call out to one another, laughing and joking. Each evening, my family would walk down the main street and talk to our neighbors. Sometimes we would even stop to get a cold soda at a little place called a buvette, which is like a snack bar. My favorite soda was one called *Pamplemousse*, which is made and bottled there in Benin, so I cannot get it here. There is no place in America like my village, Savalou.

What about you?

1. Describe the town that you consider to be your home.

_____

_____

_____

_____

2. What makes that town special to you and different from other places you have lived or visited?

_____

_____

_____

Take Action!

Get a disposable camera and make a small scrapbook of a day in the life of your town. You will want to remember these days and look back on them when you are older.

Me, age six, visiting one of the market ladies

MY MARKET DAY
ADVENTURES

Market day in our village was the event of the week. It did not really happen on the same day each week. It happened every five days according to the counting method of the Fon. It goes like this: if market day is today (hold up your right thumb) then the next market day will be in "five" days (count from index to pinky — pinky is the next market day). In America we might say that it is every four days, but I just say it's every thumb and pinky. No matter, however you count it, market day was my favorite day. On market days Mom let me start school early, then take a break and finish it after dark so that I could spend the whole day visiting my friends and bargaining.

After I had finished my required amount of school work, I would load up my wagon with water, snacks, toys, my monkey, a paigne (a cloth used to sleep on at siesta/nap time), and, usually, my brother. Clark and I took turns pulling each other while Georgie, the monkey, held onto my skirt and rode hanging there. We would start down the road toward market and walk with all the other women coming in from the smaller villages just past ours. They would tease me by calling me little mama while I would play with the small children and tickle the babies riding on their mom's back. It was about a mile walk from our house so I always liked to get going before it was too hot and come home as the sun was setting.

Once we got to market, my brother would take his allowance in order to go buy candies and new buckets for his sand box. When he finished his shopping he would stop for a yovo doko (similar to a donut) and head home. I would park my wagon near the seamstress's shop and head into the market area. The first thing I would do is walk around and see if there was anything new being sold. Next, I would decide what I needed and I would start to bargain. The key to bargaining is talking in Fon, smiling, and insulting. If you insult someone's stuff they will give you a lower price but they won't be mad. It's a funny way of making friends, but, in Benin, it works. At first, since I was a foreigner, everyone tried to get me to pay too much for things. After awhile, though, they accepted me as a member of the village and then I could get really good deals. I liked to buy from the grandmothers the best because even after we would bargain and I would buy what I wanted, they would throw in an extra gift just to be nice.

I had tons of friends at market. Sometimes I would sit with the donut lady for hours, eating donuts, talking to her customers, and dipping the donuts in sugar for her. She had a little girl about my age so we would play with my toys. When it got too hot we would grab our paignes and take a nap under the shade of the tin shelters. I also liked the Fulani women who came in from their herds to sell the cheese they made from cow's milk. They were tall, thin, had facial tattoos, and braided their hair in big braids with beads woven in. They did not speak much French or Fon but I always tried to spend time near them because I liked to watch them. Their people were nomadic so they did not stay around the area long.

Sometimes there were bad people in the market. They would try to steal money from the women selling things or steal things from the stalls. Whenever they saw foreigners, they would try to steal their wallet or purse. One day, when my friends from the capital city were visiting, a bandit opened my friend's backpack (she was a Peace Corps volunteer) and slipped out her wallet. I was watching my feet squish in the mud so I didn't look up until it was almost too late. When I did look up, I saw him pull the wallet out and I yelled BANDIT!!! He tried to run but he dropped the wallet. When it fell, I dove on it at the same time he grabbed for it. I stuffed the wallet up my shirt and grabbed his legs to slow him down until the other people in the market could help me capture him. That was a really exciting day. That day, I decided that being a spy would be a lot of fun.

$$\text{+ + + + + +}$$

What about you?
1. How do you meet people in your town?

_____

_____

_____

_____

2. What are some things you can do to meet your neighbors?

_____

_____

_____

Take Action!
Find a farmer's market near your house and visit it. Talk to the people selling things there about their items and how they made or grew them. Farmers markets are similar to African markets.

Me, age six, camel-back riding on the beach in Mombasa, Kenya

MY TRAVELS

When I returned to the USA at age nine, I could not grasp how large this country actually is. Whenever we drove anywhere I was constantly asking my parents what country we were in. You see, in West Africa, the countries are as small as some of our states. From our house in Benin we could be in Togo in an hour, Nigeria in three hours, Ghana in five hours, Burkina Faso in six hours, and Niger in seven hours. So, when we traveled, we were used to crossing international borders, not state lines. During my time in Africa, I visited seven African nations not including the ones where we had a layover on a flight. Every country was a new adventure.

Twice, my family went to Kenya. On our first visit we spent a month near the Tanzanian border, on the Masaai Mara, and in Mombasa at the beach. During our second visit we made a two-day trip north to the deserts surrounding Lake Turkana. During that trip we also visited the beach. Coming from West Africa, Kenya was paradise to me. It had malls, ice cream, and even escalators. My brother thought it was America, not Africa. In Nairobi, we stayed near the Giraffe Orphanage where we fed the giraffes by hand. While we were in Maasai land, we herded goats with some young boys, saw lions, wildebeest migration, zebras, hyenas, and tons of other wildlife. We even had traditional chai in a mud dung Maasai hut. While we were in the northern deserts of Turkana, we drove through a river in our truck (the water was so deep it came up to the door handle!), played in the mud of the riverbanks, went to a traditional goat roast, and drove across mountains on single-lane roads.

Both trips ended at Mombasa, which is a city on the coast of the Indian Ocean. The water is clear blue, and the sand is white. We had tea every afternoon by the pool, went snorkeling, and even rode in a traditional boat called a *dhow*. We traveled by the night train on the only remaining historic narrow-gauge railroad to get from Nairobi to Mombasa and back again. On the train, we had our own beds and ate our meals in the formal dining car. The taxi we took from the station to the hotel at the beach was an old-time British limo. Kenya is truly magical. I want to live in Mombasa.

Our other travels were throughout West Africa. When we went to Burkina Faso we had an accident and almost didn't get to leave the country. In Burkina Faso they had strawberries and broccoli, which we had not tasted in years. On our trip to Niger we saw wild giraffes grazing just across the border. We wilted in the 128-degree heat and shopped in the Muslim markets. One day we even took a camel trek into the Sahara Desert for a few hours. Another day we rode a pirogue down the Niger River to a village market. Our last big trip in West Africa was a tour of Togo, Ghana, and Cote D'Ivoire. Togo has old German forts and even an old German castle that are at high elevations, which make them a fun place to stay. In Ghana, we visited a rain forest with a suspended bridge system that was built throughout the middle strata of the forest. We also visited an old Portuguese fort used in the slave trade, which is where all our passports were stolen. Cote D'Ivoire was the Kenya of West Africa. We went to a hotel that had an ice rink and skated. We played in the pool of a resort, and we visited the basilica, which is an exact replica of the Vatican built in the village of Yamoussoukro, paid for by a past president of the country.

All of our travels included some stress because of police stops and border crossings. Also, there were many unsafe drivers and pedestrians that did not move for cars. We ran over quite a few piglets, goats, and chickens. Sometimes police would stop us for no reason and try to delay us until we paid a bribe. My dad never gave bribes but that meant we would often have to sit by the road in the middle of nowhere for hours until the policeman gave up on getting anything. We usually traveled in our four-wheel-drive truck. It was the only vehicle that could get through most places during the rainy season. Before we bought the truck we drove a Peugeot station wagon, but that blew up and melted the road. Luckily everyone got out in time. We also had an old Willys army jeep from World War II that we used for the first year or so. I try to see every experience in my life as an adventure, no matter where I am.

✦ ✦ ✦ ✦ ✦ ✦

What about you?

1. What is the biggest adventure you can imagine having?

_____

_____

_____

2. If you went on an adventure, when would you go and who would you want with you?

_____

_____

_____

Take Action!

Using the internet, brochures from a travel agency and travel books from the library, plan an adventure. Chose your destination and the activities to do while there. Find out about lodging, food, guides, and transportation. Estimate the cost of the whole trip. It never hurts to dream big!

Me (age 8) and some of my friends attending church together in Savalou, Benin

MY FRIENDS

The entire village of Savalou really brought me up. Even when I was only four years old, I was safe leaving my house alone. No matter where I went in the village I had dozens of Beninoise aunties and uncles watching me and keeping me out of trouble. After school each day I would go into the village until dark. I worked, played, and learned from my village friends.

There were many adults who were my friends. I already told you about the market ladies. Another friend I had was the seamstress. She made me dresses and doll clothes. She even made matching outfits for my monkey and me. She would let me sit and watch her push the pedal of her machine while I played with her extra fabric scraps. Down the road from the seamstress lived Helen, who was my best adult friend. She did not have any children yet, so she treated me like her own child. I would take naps on her floor, sweep the dirt in her courtyard with a straw broom, carry water for her, help her crush tomatoes and onions for sauce, add water to the mortar as she pounded yams, and play with my toys while she worked. When my parents left Benin, I wanted to stay and live with her and her husband.

One of my favorite friends my age was Vacencia. Her mother

came to our house a few times a week to help my mom learn to wash clothes by hand, iron with a charcoal iron, and speak Fon better. Vacencia spoke French well because her dad tutored her at home every night, so that made it easy to play with her. She taught me African games, like the jumping game, and I taught her how to do puzzles and play Memory. Christine and Christianne were twins who came over a lot, too. They liked to play dolls with me and play house in the toy kitchen by the sandbox. I'll bet they are all getting ready for marriage by now.

There were Peace Corps volunteers all over Benin. Several lived in our village or close to it. Once they met us and found out that we were pretty cool, they would stop by for an American meal, conversation in English, or just a night of pampering with a real bed and indoor shower. Kristen lived across the street. She made us funny gifts for our birthdays. Lisa came over from across town and taught us crafts. Joanne — who had to ride a moped for an hour to get to us — celebrated Jewish holidays with us and taught me Hebrew. Andrew taught at the local high school and did science projects with us like building catapults, a dam in the sand box, and satellites with mirrors. Dan and Rachel, who took a four-hour taxi ride to our house, taught us how to make batik cloth. Jennifer, who lived in a village a few hours north, quizzed us on the famous artists and masterpieces we studied and sang Christmas carols with us. I often think of serving in the Peace Corps after college because of their influence in my life.

I never wanted to leave Benin. I had a plan to just move my stuff to TinTin and Helen's house and live as their child instead of returning to a home called America that I did not know. The day before we had to leave, our village threw us a huge party. It started around 5 a.m. when they slaughtered a cow and began cooking it for the feast. During the day we had games, races, and speeches by important people. Our friends in the village had even invited our friends from neighboring towns, who were foreigners like us, to come join the farewell party. It is my last memory of having fun with all of my village.

I got to sing my favorite Fon songs, cook with the ladies, take care of the babies, color pictures with my friends, kick the soccer ball with the boys, and just enjoy my last day of being African. The next morning, when our closest friends gathered in front of our house to say good-bye, I couldn't stop crying. I was angry with my parents for making me leave. The worst part was that my friends waved and sang as we pulled out of the drive and drove away. They kept telling me I should be happy to go see my family in America because my family there missed me. I can't wait to go back to Africa. I hope I get to go soon.

What about you?

1. Who are your closest friends?

_____   _____

_____   _____

_____   _____

2. How do you choose your friends?

_____

_____

_____

_____

3. What special things do you do with your friends?

_____

_____

_____

_____

Life Rocks!

Take Action!

Make a friends scrapbook. Put in things like movie ticket stubs, photos, notes to each other, diary entries, and brochures of places you visited together, or secrets you shared. Make a copy of the scrapbook for each person. You will appreciate having the memories recorded later when you are not all together.

Part Two:
CLIMBING ROCKS!

Me (age 12) climbing "Omaha Beach" (13d) at Red River Gorge, Kentucky (photo by Mike Lordkroon)

Me, age 10, playing in the gym the month after I started climbing

GETTING STARTED

It was Christmas. I was a 10-year-old ballerina-figure skater. At that time I was skating every day for about three hours and had ballet classes nine hours per week, plus Nutcracker performance practices. Climbing was the last thing I needed to add to my schedule. It was meant to be, though. It all happened because my dad and I went to buy my mom a Christmas outfit at the mall.

We entered the mall through a sports store called Galyan's. It had just opened. At the back of the store there was a huge crowd, and we went to see what was happening. Well, as we drew closer, I could see the climbing wall, and I knew I couldn't leave until I tried it. My heart was pounding with anticipation. As we stood and watched person after person try to climb the wall, we noticed that the crowd had gathered to cheer on the climbers or to wait in line to climb themselves. We both took a number and got in line.

We soon realized that our number was about 50 off from the current number, and Dad said we wouldn't have time to wait the two or so hours for our turn. I was so bummed. About a minute later, several Marines who were at the front of the line decided to leave and on their way out they gave me their number. I was the luckiest girl alive! Now Dad couldn't say no.

41

Life Rocks!

Less than 15 minutes after that, I was on the wall. I was shaking with excitement. I just knew I could do it. The woman tied my knot and I started to climb. It was like flying. I couldn't have stopped my hands and feet from moving me up that wall if I had wanted to. I felt like I had entered a magical world all my own. Too soon, I reached the top and had to let go. I was tingling with happiness. The girl who belayed me and the guy next to her both encouraged me to keep it up. My dad just smiled politely and we finished our shopping.

I couldn't stop thinking about climbing, though. Even when I was at practices for the Nutcracker, I'd imagine myself climbing and I'd get lost in my daydream. Every day I begged to go back to Galyan's and climb. My parents took me about twice per week, and in no time at all I had conquered the challenges there and was ready for more. That was when we heard about Climb Time, a local rock climbing gym.

That Christmas break was snowy and icy. Most of the roads were impassable and we all had cabin fever. Finally, on New Year's Eve, my dad called the climbing gym to see if it was open. The guy who answered said that no one was in the gym except for him but he would stay open for us to come climb. It took us over an hour to drive the eight miles to the gym on icy roads, but it was worth it. The gym was my heaven.

We bought a membership that night and within a few weeks I had bought a chalk bag, used harness and used shoes. I also quit both ballet and skating so that I could spend all my free time climbing. Since I was homeschooled, my mom took my brother and me to climb during the days. Sometimes when we'd come in, the manager/owner, Craig, would have some new routes set just for us. It was like a game for him and for us. He was teaching us to climb, and we were solving problems on a wall. I couldn't get enough of it.

We settled into a schedule of climbing about four times per week. Two of those times were at night so my mom and dad could learn to climb, too. There were no other kids who had memberships but all the adults were very helpful and polite. I know it cramped their style a bit to have a family around, but they were good sports about it. About a month after that first climb on the Galyan's wall, we attended our first competition. It was a bouldering competition in Louisville, Kentucky, and I won the 14-and-under division. I knew then that my life had found a new course.

What about you?
1. What activities do you do that make you feel good about yourself?

_____

_____

_____

_____

2. How do you spend your free time?

_____

_____

_____

_____

Take Action!
Choose two free time activities that you have and write down why you do them and how they make you feel. If these reasons or feelings are not good, make a plan to spend more time doing things for good reasons or things that give you good feelings.

Me (age 13) climbing "Paranoia" (13b) at the Red River Gorge in Kentucky (photo by Greg Epperson)

SETTING RECORDS

Climbing outdoors is a whole different sport than gym climbing. I live about five hours from the Red River Gorge where there is enough sport climbing for a lifetime. The problem is that I only get down there about two times per year because my family does not climb, plus my brother plays football and that takes up most of the good climbing weekends in the fall. I enjoy climbing on real rocks. I love heights, and real rocks can go pretty high. One of the highlights of my outdoor experiences happened when I became the youngest female to onsight a 13a, which is a very high difficulty rating for an outdoor climb.

Now that you know the ending, I'll give you the story. When I was 11, my hero, Katie Brown, came to coach me for about a week. She spent time in the gym teaching me to use my head and not just my muscles. She did fun things like blindfold climbing, a game called beep and she worked with me on footwork. While she was here she stayed at my house so I got to ask her questions about being a famous climber and how she kept her priorities straight. I admire her because she went to college, and she did other things like run marathons in addition to climbing.

At the end of her visit, we visited the Red River Gorge in

Slade, Kentucky, for a few days. The first thing she realized was that I was a big talker about heights because I really was afraid to fall. She would put me on routes where I had to think, and then she would let me climb until I fell. No matter how upset I was about falling, she would tell me to get back on the rock and keep trying. I am sure everyone within earshot thought I was the biggest baby ever to climb.

It was May and the weather felt like December. We hadn't brought enough warm clothes. The rain and sleet pelted our camper all night. The days were damp and dreary. Everything felt wrong. In my memory, the rock was cold and wet and the hikes were muddy and long every day that weekend. I really wanted to show Katie that I wasn't a wimp, but I wasn't getting any help from nature.

To be perfectly honest, I was not a very nice person most of that trip. I really do not like to fail at anything, and for the first few days, all I did was fail. I felt like I would never be able to climb a hard route outside. I whined because of the cold and I cried when I fell. I pouted when I didn't want to do a route that looked too hard, and I was mean to everyone who tried to encourage me. I am amazed Katie stuck it out. Actually, though, it was her gentleness that kept me going. She was firm, but kind, and she believed in me.

Our last day there, I woke up feeling really sick. My throat hurt and I had a fever. I had set my sights on this route named Harvest at the cliff area called the Motherload. The rating of Harvest was currently set at 13a because several holds had broken in key spots making it harder to climb, and that level of difficulty excited me. Also, I liked the look of the route. People rarely climbed this route so I had no info on it being good, bad, hard to reach, or anything else. It was a route that I chose on instinct only.

I hiked in and warmed up on a few routes to the right. My last warm-up was on my favorite route called Chainsaw Massacre. My hands and arms felt loose and strong, and that feeling put me in a good mood. I went to get ready while Katie hung the draws (put up the safety clips I would use for attaching my rope as I climbed) on Harvest. I came back, tied in to my rope, and started climbing. As I passed each draw, my breathing regulated and my head cleared. At one point, I had to really search for a good hold and I almost panicked, but all the practice falling calmed me. I knew I was safe even if I didn't succeed. There were five other people there that day and they all stopped to watch me. I knew I wouldn't fail. When I clipped the 13th draw and the anchors at the top I wanted to cry with joy. I had faced my fear and conquered my attitude. The route was mine.

✦ ✦ ✦ ✦ ✦ ✦

What about you?
1. What are some of your personal victories?

_____

_____

_____

_____

2. How can you encourage someone you know to reach his or her potential?

_____

_____

_____

_____

Take Action!
   Sit down with a friend and set goals for this week, this month, this season, and this year. Show them to each other so you can push each other to keep working hard.

Life Rocks!

Autumn (middle) and Lauren (right) hanging out with their mentor, me (age 14)

BEING A ROLE MODEL

There I was, telling the TV camera how much I loved to climb and laughing at the commentator's jokes. Within hours of that program's airing, my email inbox bulged with letters from girls across the USA who wanted my autograph or had questions for me. Since then, I have responded to thousands of emails from youth all over the world. At first I thought it was fun, sort of like signing autographs at events. After a few weeks, though, I realized that these kids looked up to me. I was a teenage role model. That scared me a little. More than that, though, it inspired me to live a life worth modeling.

Climbing was the first area where I worked on being a role model. Initially, I volunteered as an assistant team and club coach so I could get to know young climbers and they could get to know me. For four hours a week I would belay and encourage climbers ages 3-13 of all abilities. Then I spent time at an inner- city recreation center encouraging youth who were on outings to a small climbing wall in a warehouse. Now, I focus my time on three young girls who train 10-12 hours per week. Being a role model in the climbing gym challenges me to have a good attitude at all times as well as a strong work ethic. I am a mentor to one of these girls. I talk to her about things beyond climbing, and I challenge her to be a leader in

49

all areas of her life. Whether I am coaching, mentoring or training, I am being watched, and I know that my behavior is being copied by youth around me.

My achievements and attitude on and off the wall have earned me the opportunity to be a speaker at all kinds of gatherings of youth across the USA. I have spoken to church groups, graduations, antidrug weeks, school assemblies, honors banquets, and much more. I speak honestly about the challenges I face in my life. I tell them about the pressures of making the right choices and the guidelines I use in order to make choices wisely. I would be a fake if I spoke about these things and then lived my life very differently. That does not make saying no to peer pressure any easier for me, but I value the respect others have for me so I often go against the crowd to stand up for what I believe is right.

Sometimes being a role model involves hard choices in areas such as what I wear or how I talk. I make sure that the clothes I choose to wear in public are clothes that reflect my values and the values that I am modeling for other young people. Even though these are often not the most "trendy" styles that other teens are wearing, they are appropriate. Also, when I am on the road, I do not get much sleep. This can make me grouchy. I have to be careful not to act disrespectfully toward my parents in these situations. There have even been situations at competitions where my competitors have been extremely rude to me or the results have not been what I had hoped they would be. People watch me carefully particularly in these types of situations, and so I make sure to overlook the rudeness of others or hold my head high when I really feel like crying.

There is no place more challenging to be a role model than in the halls of my school. It is there where I am tempted to act a certain way to get a boy's attention or to fit into the popular group. Last fall, I even went through a phase where I wanted to stop packing my lunch and just buy school lunches so I could fit in. After two days of this, my stomach was upset and my athletic performances were suffering. So, I began packing celery and peanut butter again. As soon as I showed back up with my lunch box, several other athletes came up to tell me how I had inspired them to pack a healthy lunch so they could perform better in their sports, too. Through that experience I realized that even the smallest things don't go unnoticed. Therefore, I have just decided to be me (bright yellow lunch box and all). Those who appreciate who I am will be my friends, and the others are probably going to be bad influences anyway so I don't worry about them anymore.

What about you?
1. How do you choose your role models?

_____

_____

_____

_____

2. Who looks up to you? Why?

_____

_____

_____

3. What are some things that you could change that would make you a better role model?

_____

_____

_____

Life Rocks!

Take Action!

Keep a journal for a month about role models. Write down things you admire in others, and write down all the people who tend to hang around you or admire you. Write down anything you do that might be something you want (or don't want) people to copy. Be aware; people are watching you.

Self-portrait (age 12) snapped with a disposable camera 2,000 feet up The Nose

CLIMBING THE NOSE

I blame Hans Florine. It was all his idea. I had actually never even heard of The Nose, nor had I ever been to Yosemite before 2001. Hans called one day in April 2001 and asked me if I wanted to try and climb this big rock with him and a few other people. I found out later that it would take up to four days to climb it. It took my parents and me several weeks to decide if I should do it. Even after we decided I would go, we kept wondering if it really was a good idea. I was only 12, and I would be up there without my parents. What if something went wrong? You don't just get hurt out there, you can die. Well, once we started climbing there was no turning back. I was on my way **UP** — about 3,000 feet up.

For the next five months, I prepared. I had never climbed on limestone rock so I tried to get experience on rock that was limestone, or similar to it. That meant traveling and camping quite a bit over the summer. Also, I had never done a type of climbing called crack climbing. This means you climb up a crack in the rock by literally jamming your fingers, hands, arms, legs…whatever fits, into the crack. You jam your body part into the crack in such a way that it gets stuck enough so you can use it as leverage to move your body up to a higher point to jam again. In preparation for this, I practiced taping my hands to reduce scraping. I also practiced climbing short cracks on rock in Kentucky to get the hang of how to jam effectively. Finally, I worked on my endurance so that I could climb and pull up my gear for over eight hours each day.

I flew to Yosemite several days before the climb was scheduled to begin so I could cram in last-minute practice on actual Yosemite limestone. I also wanted to hang out with the people who were going to be my teammates. I stayed with Hans and his wife, Jaqueline, and their little girl, Marianna. They took me out on 300- to 400-foot training climbs each morning, and we spent the afternoons swimming in the waterhole. At night, Hans helped me pack while he convinced my dad that I really would be safe. My dad continued to doubt his decision. Luckily, my Uncle Tom came out from Colorado to keep Dad company and to distract him. His presence made the last- minute preparations less stressful for me. I already had a lot to think about.

The day we started the three-day push to the top, everyone was excited and edgy. We did not know each other very well, so we were working on communication as well as the logistics of getting food, clothes, ropes, gear, water, cameras, and packs for seven people up the wall. There were some disagreements over little things like the necessity and weight of can openers versus teddy bears as well as who would carry what. I was nervous and tried not to cry when I said good-bye to my dad. He stood in the field all that day with binoculars watching us climb. At night we slept on rock ledges with our harnesses on, clipped to safety ropes. My dad had a walkie-talkie, and he would talk to me each night before I fell asleep. The climbing was hard. It was hot and windy so I was literally blown out of the crack and across the wall several times. Sometimes, the cracks were so small that they pinched my fingers when I pushed them in. My arms ached from pulling bags of gear and water up after each climb. It was a huge challenge.

Early on the third day we reached the false summit. After this point, the rock face ends and there is a steep path to the true summit that takes another half hour for us to hike. We took group photos and then the team split. Hans and I hiked to the true summit to add a rock to the summit pile and to sign the book up there while the rest of the team started down another path. My dad and Uncle Tom were waiting for us at the top. I literally fell into my dad's arms and cried with relief. It had been the hardest three days of my life. It was about a seven-mile hike down the backside of the Nose to get to the cars and get home. Luckily, Hans, Dad, and Uncle Tom carried most of the gear. They each had over 80 pounds of gear going down.

That night I swam, slept, and tried to tell my dad all that happened. There had been a video team up there with us to make a documentary of the whole experience. Over the next days we got to watch portions of the film. It was fun to sit and laugh about all our adventures on the wall. The morning after our climb, two planes hit the World Trade Center towers, while one hit the Pentagon, and life in America changed. Dad and I couldn't get flights out of California so we took our rental car and drove straight through for three days to get home. I know that three days pulling my body and gear straight up 3,000 feet was much more fun than the three days riding 3,000 miles east in a car.

What about you?
1. What has been the biggest challenge in your life?

_____

_____

_____

_____

Life Rocks!

2. What did you learn from that challenge?

_____

_____

_____

3. What would you change about what you did?

_____

_____

_____

Take Action!

Read a book about someone doing something you have always wanted to do.

X-Games 2002: I won gold in speed climbing at age 14
(photo by ESPN/Chazzom/Tony Donaldson)

WINNING THE X-GAMES

Katie Brown is my hero. Katie was the first American woman to win a gold medal in climbing at the X-Games. In fact, she won several times while she was in her teens. At that time, the X-Games had difficulty climbing as well as speed climbing, and later, they even had bouldering. I did not know about her wins until several years after they happened, but I was still very impressed. Katie inspired me. After meeting Katie and hearing and reading about her accomplishments, I decided that I, too, wanted to compete in the X-Games. The only problem was, no one at the X-Games would take me seriously when I wrote letters asking for an opportunity to compete. Meanwhile, the X-Games dropped difficulty climbing and then bouldering from the event list. So, my only chance of getting to the X-Games was to work on my speed climbing.

Finally, in 2002, the X-Game climbing organizers announced that a gym in California was holding a national speed-climbing competition and the winner would get invited to the X-Games that summer in Philadelphia. I trained several times per week at a 45-foot wall in Galyans. I was bummed the week of the competition, though, because I came down with the stomach flu. I thought my chances were gone. I flew out to try and compete anyway. I am glad I did because when I got out there ready to climb, I was so excited that I didn't feel weak at all. I climbed very fast and I ended up winning. For the next four months, I trained even harder. During training, I hit my knee so many times on protruding holds that I still have a scar. At times it was very frustrating, and it would be hard not to take my feelings out on my parents. Basically, I had no idea how to train properly. The Russian and Asian women who were going to be my competitors were professional speed climbers. I tried to put that knowledge out of my mind and just focus on my own skills.

In Philadelphia, during the two days before the finals, I had a chance to practice on the actual 65-foot X-Games wall. Each competitor got about 30 minutes a day to train and get used to the wall. The holds were placed pretty far apart so it forced us all to jump from hold to hold. When my turns came it was as if my arms had turned to jello and there was grease on my shoes. I kept falling off and when I didn't fall, I clocked the slowest times of all the competitors. I began worrying about making a fool of myself. My dad saw my disappointment and sensed my stress, so he took me sight-seeing and encouraged me to take in all the other events. He wanted me to just enjoy this once-in-a-lifetime experience no matter if I won or lost.

The morning of the actual competition, Hans Florine, a previous X-Games and world champion speed climber who was staying with my dad and me, greeted me at breakfast by congratulating me on winning. I thought he had lost his mind. He had seen one of my practices and everyone had heard about the other. I was so shocked at his words that I just thanked him and finished eating. I hurried to get to the wall for my final practice session and then a day full of single-elimination races. My practice was not any better than the previous ones, so at this point I decided to simply enjoy the experience and not stress about the upcoming races.

My qualifying time put me near the middle of the pack, so my first race was against someone who had almost the same time. I barely won that race, and I moved on to the semifinals.

After winning that race as well, I faced a very fast Russian woman for the finals. The butterflies in my stomach almost paralyzed me. It was the chants of the crowd and the cheers of my grandma (Nana), who was in the front row, that motivated me. The starter asked us to approach the wall, and then the gun went off. I felt like I was flying. It was the greatest feeling in the world. When I hit the buzzer, looked back, and saw I had won, I cried and cheered at the same time.

Since that day, my life has been a blur of exciting opportunities. I have been on talk shows and game shows. My picture has shown up on magazine covers and in books. I have traveled to several states and all over Indiana giving talks to youth about making good choices and reaching for their dreams. I have lobbied in Washington D.C., on behalf of Title IX to protect the opportunities of girls in sports as well as for PE for Life, which is a new type of PE program that teaches people how to be healthy through noncompetitive activities. I know things will be normal again soon, but for now, winning the X-Games has been like being crowned princess for a year, and I am enjoying every minute of it.

What about you?

1. What is the biggest thing you can think of doing or accomplishing in your life?

_____

_____

_____

2. Who is the one person in the world who believes in that dream with you?

_____

_____

_____

_____

Life Rocks!

3. How would your life change if that dream came true?

_____

_____

_____

_____

Take Action!

Look at people you admire who are superstars in sports or some other thing. Find out how they are impacting their community, nation, and the world by using their fame to get a message across about a certain cause or idea. After doing this research, choose your role models wisely by choosing people who are generous and caring and are impacting the world.

Clark and me (ages 10 and 12), also known as batboy and batgirl, playing in the gym soon after our family bought it

BUYING A GYM

When I started climbing, I climbed in a gym that had a cold cement floor, shredded rubber in the landing areas by the walls, and was filled with black dust from the climber's chalk mixed with residue from the rubber. After a few years climbing in this gym, it changed owners. The new owner didn't do things the same way as the old owner, and the new ways were not making the gym money. In fact, within a year, the gym was in financial trouble and my parents were worried about it closing. About that time, my dad was finishing his MBA and had written a business plan for a climbing gym as his thesis. The more my parents talked about it, the more it made sense to buy the struggling gym and try to add life to it again.

After about five months of negotiations, the gym became ours. No, there is not a lot of money in owning a climbing gym in Indiana, but since my family had been missionaries up until then, we were used to living simply. Plus, this was an opportunity to work together as a family, and that appealed to all of us. The first thing we did was remodel the whole gym. We repainted walls, ordered thousands of new holds, built a pro shop and locker room, cleaned the bathrooms, and added a balcony for parties. We even took out the shredded tire. That was the worst mess because we had to rent a mini bulldozer to scoop it. After it was out, we put in a padded floor. My idea was to add a closed-in area where toddlers could climb around without getting hurt or getting in the way of the other climbers. We added that, too. All of these changes brought in a lot of new business, so the gym survived instead of closing.

After about a year with the first gym, my dad thought we should open another gym on the other side of town to give us relief from overcrowded weekends. We found a suitable space inside a gymnastics facility. It was smaller than our first gym but 12 feet taller. Within three months the walls were built and painted, the padded floor was in, and the gym was open. I loved that gym because it was tall, so I could practice long routes and work on my endurance. Plus, it was not very crowded at first, so when I wanted to train in peace, I could climb there. Luckily, a man named David came along to manage the gym so that my dad was not spending 80 hours a week running both gyms. David added an upstairs climbing area and an observation balcony. It's really cool.

One of the best things about owning these gyms is the chance to help at competitions, climbing clinics, slide shows by explorers, and other special events. When we have competitions, it is more fun to stay at the gym all night helping set and test routes than it is to climb in the competition. I have gotten the opportunity to meet many famous climbers who come in to do clinics or slide shows. Usually they stay at our house or at least my dad takes them out to dinner. I have played climbing games with my hero, Katie Brown, played fooseball with superstar Obe Carrion, gotten sponsor advice from adventurer Roxanna Brock, and many more. I also get to hang out on busy Saturdays cheering little kids up the wall, checking safety knots of first-time climbers, and belaying for worn-out parents during birthday parties.

Sure, owning a climbing gym means I can climb as much as I want, whenever I want. It also means that some of my friends have worked there. Most of all it means my family gets to be together a lot. We can have a family dinner even if my parents are working because we just take it to the gym and eat on the balcony. I have learned what it takes to be a good employee by watching my dad deal with both good and bad workers. My brother and I appreciate money because we see firsthand what it takes to make money. My dad's paycheck does not magically appear; we know exactly where that money comes from and how hard we all worked to get it. I am proud that my family owns these gyms. More than anything else, I hope that we have made the gyms a fun place for families to hang out and have adventures together, just like us!

What about you?

1. What do you appreciate about your family?

_____

_____

_____

2. What do you do to help your parents out each day?

_____

_____

_____

3. How does your life make you unique?

_____

_____

_____

Take Action!

Find out about what your parents do for work. Learn about how many hours they work each week, when, what they do, and what they think are the hardest and best parts of their jobs. Write a letter to your parents telling them how much you appreciate how hard they work in order to give you the life you have.

*Me, age 13, playing games in isolation with Kate and Lauren
before the final round of the Junior National Championships. (All
three of us made the U.S. Junior Team!)*

COMPETING FOR FUN

America is the land of competitive sports. Indianapolis is the amateur sports capital of the world. Climbing is becoming a highly competitive, amateur sport faster than any other sport in the U.S. With this rise in popularity comes a rise in poor behavior on and off the wall by everyone involved in the sport. Since I started when I was 10, until now, I have seen an increase in bad attitudes and inappropriate emotional outbursts by competitors, parents and spectators. I, for one, hope that these will not continue to increase, and that everyone will step back and get a perspective on the nature of competitive climbing and on youth sports in general.

For the past three years, the youth arm of the USCCA (United States Competition Climbing Association) has been giving sportsmanship awards to the athletes who have the best attitudes on and off the wall. I have won this award all three years. It is a great honor because it is something that is voted on by my climbing peers and not by adults in a room somewhere. I don't set out to win the award, but I do set out to try to make every competition a fun experience for myself and for those around me — both competitors and spectators.

In order to make the competitions fun for myself I begin by training hard. When I am lazy with my training, it makes me uptight about competing instead of happy. What makes me even more uncomfortable than not training is not knowing what is going on at a competitive event or being unprepared. The night before the competition I pack and double-check my bag of gear so I don't stress myself out by forgetting something. I make sure I have read and undertood all the rules for that particular event. When I arrive, I make sure I am rested and fed and that I have food and drink to tide me over until the event is finished. As soon as I enter the gym or competition area, I think only positive things about the people around me. I especially make sure not to compare myself to them. I go into each experience planning to make a new friend by the end of it. Throughout the competition, I try not to be aware of the performance of others. I remind myself that my competition is myself or even the route setters. No matter how mean or nasty I am or how many bad things I say about someone else, climbing is not tennis and I cannot force my competitors to make an error. If my best is not as good as their best the only thing I can do is train harder for next time.

The thing that always surprises me is how stressed-out everyone is at a competition. I try to alleviate some of that stress by having fun. When I am competing as an adult, I have to make sure not to disrupt someone else's mental preparation by having too much fun or by being too loud. That would be inconsiderate of me. But, I can always find someone in isolation to play a card game with me or draw pictures or even play yo-yo. Sometimes I bring a bottle of bubbles or a beach ball into isolation as a diversion. I have found that most adults welcome this change of pace and end up having a really good time hanging out before competing. This is even more true at youth competitions. I make it a point to try to find younger or more inexperienced competitors and distract them so they don't get nervous. If they are busy playing climbing games or UNO and then their turn is called, they are more reluctant about stopping whatever we are dong to have fun than they are nervous about their upcoming climb.

Since my parents have been sitting through competitions all over North America for several years, I have a pretty good feeling for the spectator's fun factor. One thing I try to never do is cry when I don't do well. I remind myself that there are people in the audience who would have been thrilled to have even made it to the point where I am. If I cry over not placing or climbing well, I feel like I am being selfish about winning rather than appreciative about the whole experience. If I get to the top of a route I wave to the crowd and smile. If I fall, I turn to the crowd, shrug, and still smile. I talk to people near me while I am waiting to climb. I take time to sign autographs and I try to be myself — silly. One year I even shot silly string at the cameramen at the Gorge Games. Sometimes I put a stuffed monkey at the top of a route and throw it out if I get there. In all, I try to let the spectators have as much fun as I am having by sharing my experience with them. After I climb, I make sure to go into the crowd and talk to little girls, answer questions, sign autograph, and just let people see I am a normal person like them. Hopefully, one of these days, another little girl will meet me and will be inspired to dream big, too.

What about you?

1. How do you keep a good attitude when you play a sport or pursue a hobby?

_____

_____

_____

_____

2. How do you help others enjoy doing that activity with you?

_____

_____

_____

Life Rocks!

3. How are you a leader, or an example, to people you meet every day?

_____

_____

_____

Take Action!

Write five ways, you can be a better sport in the game of life.

Me at age 12 practicing climbing on the climbing wall at my house in what used to be our guest room

EARNING
OPPORTUNITIES

I have always been active. As a nine-year-old girl I practiced axels and cartwheels on the soccer field when the ball was at the other end because it drove me nuts to stand there watching everyone else but me run around. My brother and I still make up crazy games and obstacle courses using all the sports items we can think of. Our most famous creation involved the idea of carnival rides. It wound inside and outside of the house and used everything from laundry baskets and sleeping bags to the roof top and roller blades. All this energy is a big help to me in sports, especially in rock climbing. But, more than just being an outlet for my extra energy, my involvement in climbing has made me a better person even when I am not speed climbing blindfolded or doing some other silly trick.

A big saying in our house is "use your opportunities wisely." My parents are not competitive parents. The first thing they ask my brother and me when we get done with a game or competition is, "Did you have fun?" Because of their example, we know that participating in sports is first and foremost a chance for us to meet new people and to be role models. So, if we go out and act snooty or mean so that others don't want to be around us, we have lost that opportunity. There have been times in my climbing career when my parents have made me take a break from training and competing because I was getting so focused on beating "so-and-so" that I was not pleasant to be around. I am glad they did that. Through these breaks, I learned that climbing should always be fun and I should only compete against myself, not another person.

Another thing that is important in our family is the idea that you earn opportunities. You see, just because you are good at something in our house does not mean that you automatically get to have new gear or go on trips for your sport. My parents believe that you earn these things through effort. For example, just because I qualified to compete in the X-Games last year, did not mean that I was automatically going to them. I had to sit down and make a training plan and set goals to prove to my parents that this was important to me and I was willing to sacrifice for it. This process helped me realize that everyone in my family has to sacrifice time and money for my opportunities. Not taking things for granted has taught me to appreciate the fact that I can even be involved in sports in the first place. It has also shown me the importance of setting goals and living a healthy lifestyle in order to be a better athlete.

Finally, I know that if I am not doing my best to train and prepare for competition, then I will lose my opportunity to someone who is working harder than me. Sure, it gets old climbing in the same old gym four days a week year-round. There are even times when I just want to go in and goof around rather than work out. Yet, I know that if I goof off, I could get hurt and then I would lose everything. Plus, if I get lazy, then I will not reach my personal goals. I don't want that to happen because it feels so good to succeed no matter if that success is getting to the top of a particular wall or learning a new skill. In climbing, just like in life, opportunities are limited. Not everyone can be a leader, a champion, or a captain, yet everyone wants those titles. It is the person who works the hardest toward the goal who gets it. When I was 10 years old, I called the organizers of the X-Games begging them to let me compete. They laughed at me, but didn't change my goal. I worked every day with my eyes set on going to the X-Games and winning. Three years later I did just that. Perseverance pays off no matter what you are doing.

Rock climbing has been a great way for me to grow up and learn how to live like a champion. I don't just set goals for my climbing; I set them in school, in hobbies, and in other projects like writing this book. Also, I do not let quitting enter my mind as an option. I just look at the positive and keep working toward that goal I have set, no matter how impossible or far off it might seem. By training with a wide variety of people and competing both as a youth and an adult I have learned the value of helping others, not just beating them. True competition is more than a medal; it is the feeling you get from performing at your best because you have trained and prepared to do just that. At the end of the day, whether I am a professional climber, a kindergarten teacher, a lawyer or a spy when I grow up, I will always use these lessons from climbing to keep things in perspective.

What about you?

1. In what situations do you feel the most pressure to compete?

_____

_____

_____

_____

2. How do you handle that pressure?

_____

_____

_____

_____

Life Rocks!

3. What are your personal goals?

_____

_____

_____

_____

4. What makes you feel like quitting?

_____

_____

_____

_____

Take Action!

Write down three goals for your life. Under those goals write a promise to yourself not to compare your progress to anyone else and not to quit. Post this paper where you can see it every day. Reward yourself when you reach your goals.

Me at age 13 with professional climber Obe Carrion, who is also my training buddy

MAKING FRIENDS

During the first years of my climbing career, my brother and I were the only kids in the gym who climbed on a regular basis. The other kids who came in were there for birthday parties or Cub Scout group meetings. The adults in the gym were very helpful and kind to us. They let us climb with them on the bouldering walls and they taught us new moves. It wasn't that we were lonely, we just felt like we were cramping the adults' ways a bit. Occasionally a cuss word would slip out of their mouth and they would apologize to us. Sometimes they would forget we were there and start talking about things we didn't need to hear. After awhile, I decided that it was time to get more kids into climbing so we could have people our own age to hang out with and the adults could have their space back.

With the help of my mom I made posters and fliers to put around the gym. I hung around on the weekends and handed out information to all the party kids and Cub Scouts. I talked to the gym owner and some of the adult climbers and arranged a time for the kids to meet as a club. The adult climbers volunteered to come to the club meetings twice per month and help the kids learn the basics of climbing. It was a perfect plan until the club reached over 50 kids and there wasn't enough room in the gym to host them all at once. Fortunately, about that time, half of the club kids split off to form a team of kids who met more often, went to competitions, and wanted to take their skills to the next level. Finally, the gym was hopping with youth, and Clark and I had plenty of young people to climb with. I am not sure if the adults were entirely thrilled, though, because their techno and hip-hop music was now interspersed with Disney soundtracks and N'Sync ballads. To their credit, they accepted the changes without complaining.

It was fun to have a group of kids from our gym to travel to competitions with. There is this organization called the USCCA and it organizes a nationwide youth climbing series that culminates in a national championship. It even selects a youth national climbing team. Our gym team traveled around the Midwest competing and having fun. Through these competitions I met kids from all over the USA. Two of my best buddies are a hip-hop dancer/climber from Berkeley, California, and a field hockey player/climber from Colorado Springs, Colorado. I met them at national competitions as my competitors, but after three days in isolation playing games and trying to relax, we ended up much more than competitors. Some of the greatest times I have had outside of competitions were my outdoor climbing trips with the youth I met at competitions. Honestly, without my friends Kenny and Jeremy egging me on and laughing at me when I was scared, I probably would never have learned to enjoy outdoor climbing.

Over this past year I have also traveled and competed internationally, which has opened even more doors to me. At the Gorge Games I met climbers from Canada. At the X-Games I made friends from Venezuela, Russia, Indonesia, and Australia. The Youth World Championships, with 42 nations represented, were the best, though. I have more email pals than I can count from over 13 nations. I email my friends weekly. We exchange training tips, funny stories, and photos of our climbing adventures. Best of all, when they travel to the USA or I go to their country we get to meet up and climb together. It's been so much fun sharing my sport and my culture in this way.

Even though I have climbing friends scattered across the globe, the friends that are the most important to me are the ones who are my training buddies. Training buddies are climbers who climb when you climb. They are close to your level but don't have to be exactly the same. The most important thing to look for in a training buddy is confidence and fun. Training buddies should never compare themselves to one another. They just motivate each other to climb harder and smarter. I have had a few special training buddies over the years. The one who inspired me the most was Obe Carrion, who is a professional adult climber. He lowers himself to my level to climb with me to make me a better climber. He was my training buddy for a year. I am so lucky!

What about you?

1. How do you meet friends through your activities?

_____

_____

_____

_____

2. What is special about the friends you meet in this way?

_____

_____

_____

_____

3. Do you have training buddies in your sports or hobbies?

_____

_____

_____

_____

Life Rocks!

Take Action!

Meet five new people through your activities this year who are not from your team or club. Get their email and start building friendships with them. Try to make friends with people who enjoy what you do, yet who appear to be very different from you. You'll be surprised how deceiving looks can be.

Part Three:
SCHOOL ROCKS!

Me (age 14) studying for exams in the airport on the way to a competition

Me (age 14) sporting my high school varsity letter jacket

I AM AFRAID OF THE DARK

Just talk to my brother and he'll tell you all about how annoying I can be. I talk too much. I make up words when I can't think of one that goes with what I want to say. When I am in public, I talk too loudly. If people look familiar, I will go up to them and ask them how I know them, and they are usually not who I think they are. I even get huge pimples on the end of my nose and have lots of horrible hair days. I am as normal as they come.

Even though I am very talented at a few sports, namely figure skating, pole vaulting, and rock climbing, I am clueless about every other sport. Guys at my school think that ESPN should hire me to commentate on sports because I mix up the rules of all the different sports so much that it gets really funny (for them, that is. I don't even realize I do it.). For example, at a basketball game recently, when our team was ahead by two points and there were nine seconds left on the clock, I stood up in front of hundreds of fans and yelled, "Take a knee!" How was I supposed to know that you could only do that in football? Another time a friend told me she played catcher on the softball team and I asked, "Which one?" because I thought everyone caught the ball and so they were all catchers. When it comes to sports, I have learned to watch and learn. I have a lot to learn because they didn't have anything but soccer in Benin.

I have also been known to completely embarrass myself at the worst times. The most recent episode happened in the weight room at school. I was working out for track while the varsity baseball team was also working out. When we all finished we sat around for few minutes to talk about things like prom dates and cars. Well, I was sitting on the bench that had leg weights that you hook your toes under and lift by straightening your legs in order to work on your quad (thigh) muscles. I was feeling a bit proud of my muscles, and I wanted to show the guys how strong I was. So, I hooked my toes under the weights without even checking how heavy they were and straightened my legs, thus lifting the weights. All of a sudden, my knees felt funny and when I tried to let the weights back down, my knees wouldn't bend. As hard as I tried to bend my knees I couldn't get them to move in order to give my muscles a break. Two seconds later, my muscles relaxed but my knees didn't bend so my body was thrown forward onto the floor and I landed on my face in the middle of the entire baseball team. I don't remember saying anything but I know that I laughed and worked my way to the door as fast as possible.

Aside from having a negative sports IQ and having a habit of embarrassing myself, I have also never been invited to a school dance. Since I was homeschooled until high school, I had never gotten to go to any sort of school dance function. Therefore, when I got to high school, all I could think of was going to a dance in a beautiful dress. No one knew me my freshman year, so I didn't get asked to the Homecoming dance. By Christmas dance, I was fed up with waiting to be asked so I invited someone from my church to go with me. For the Valentine's dance, I went with a group of girls instead of a date. Over the next summer I got my hopes set on going to the Homecoming dance so my mom even arranged our trip to France for the Junior World Climbing Championships around the dance dates. Well, first of all, I did not get asked so I called a friend from out of state to take me, and then the dance was rescheduled due to weather conditions. The new date was in the middle of my trip to France. I had no luck at either the Christmas or the Valentine's dances this year as well and I think I was the only sophomore girl in the world who didn't get invited to prom. I'm starting to wonder if I just wasn't meant to go to these dances.

Really, what I am trying to say is that I am just like you. I drive my brother crazy. I forget my homework. I get sick. I don't like doing my chores. While we are being honest, I might as well tell you that I really am afraid of the dark, too. My nightly routine to protect me from the Boogie Man in my room is very detailed. First I have to turn on all the lights and look in all the corners and under my piled-up clothes to make sure nothing is hiding there. Then I have to check in my closets and close them tightly. After that, I leap from the closets to the bed and I turn on my radio so I won't hear any scary noises. I hug my sleep monkey (Gorgie) under my arm, call my mom, and turn off the light. Then my mom comes in and rubs my back until I am almost asleep. That way, when she closes my door, I don't imagine that all the creepy shadows are the Boogie Man's babies. I know, I'm silly.

What about you?

1. What do you think are the things that make you normal?

_____

_____

_____

2. What is one embarrassing moment or secret fear that you haven't told anyone?

_____

_____

_____

_____

Life Rocks!

Take Action!

List all the things that you get teased for, wish you could change about yourself, are afraid of, and wish you did better. Now, cut up that list and make a collage of you out of the pieces. All those things make you special. Face them, don't hide them.

Me (age 13) practicing pole vault for the 2002 Junior Olympics, which I won and set the national 12/13 record

I POLE VAULT

When I was nine years old I went to the state fair. Along one of the side streets there was a rug of rubber rolled out and guys with long sticks were lined up to run down the rug and fling themselves up over a bar balanced between two other poles. I was enthralled. I stopped and watched them until the last guy couldn't run anymore. I wanted to do that! What a great feeling they must have, I thought, soaring through the air and free-falling from that height onto squishy pads. I couldn't get that desire to fly out of my mind, so, for three years I bugged my mom to let me try.

My mom usually lets me try anything I want as long as I finish what I start, and I only try a few things at a time so I can give my best effort to each thing. The more I bugged her the more she realized that I was serious. As we looked into it, though, we realized that this was not going to be easy. Pole vaulting, even though it had officially debuted as a women's event at the 1996 Summer Olympics, and a U.S. woman had won in '96 and 2000, was still not recognized as a women's event in Indiana high schools. As we called around and talked to coaches, everyone told us the same thing. It's not a girls' event; maybe in a few years. I didn't want to wait a few years so we called USA Track and Field and they recommended a coach in the area who might consider working with me. We called and met with him. At that meeting he gave me videos and drill pages and told me to go home and work with a wooden six foot pole. I was to come back in a few weeks to show him my progress.

Three weeks later, I went back to him and I guess he could see how hard I had worked because he let me start training with his high school vaulters even though I was only 12 years old. It was hard for me. I made progress but it was slow and incremental. Sometimes I would make no progress for a whole week. Since every other athletic thing I had ever tried had come easily to me and I had progressed very quickly, I had to work hard not to be discouraged. By the end of seven months, I was consistently vaulting over eight feet but I could not bend my pole and, if I wanted to go any higher, I had to figure out a way to do that.

When I started high school that next fall, I found out that there was a new pole vault coach at my school. He had coached the boys' state vault champion from the previous three years, and he had transferred to my school. I couldn't believe my luck. Yet, I was also really nervous because I didn't want him to take one look at my vault abilities and give up on me. He was patient, though. He started me on a conditioning program that was tough. He even told me that I was weak, which really motivated me. I am the strongest girl I know; how could he say that? Once I began training, I found out what he meant; vaulters have to be more than just strong, they have to be elite.

By January, I was bending my pole and ready for an even bigger pole. I was still only vaulting 8½ feet but I was faster and stronger than I had ever been. Then, between mid-February and mid-March I cleared 9 feet, 9½ feet, 10 feet, and 10½ feet! All the hard work was paying off. My real goal for the year was to win the freshman county meet against the boys. I didn't just want to beat the boys, I wanted people in Indiana to know that girls could vault, too, and that they should have their own event.

My next two months were spent perfecting my technique in every area of my vault and getting even stronger and faster. I won every freshman meet I entered, but more importantly, I earned the respect of the other guy vaulters. At first they would laugh at me or think that I'd be no competition. After a few minutes of warming up, though, they would see I was a serious athlete and we would begin to relate on equal ground.

The week of the freshman county meet was cold and rainy. I knew some of the other guys around the county were improving rapidly, but I tried to focus solely on my own progress and technique. I had a chance of winning only if stopped worrying about all the other vaulters. The night of the meet there were over 15 vaulters. I was the only girl. By the time I started at nine feet there were seven boys still left. At 10 feet there were five, and three of us made it to 10 ½ feet. We all missed at 10 ½ feet so we had to go to sudden death at 10'3". The first guy missed. I was up. I closed my eyes, pictured a perfect vault, told myself I could do it and that I deserved to win, opened my eyes, rocked back into position, lifted my pole, and began to run. Everything from there was automatic. I let my body do it all. It felt perfect. I sailed over the bar and hit the mat. As I looked up, the bar was still on the standards and I jumped to my feet with a shout. The last guy still had to vault, but I didn't care. I was still in. In the end, the last guy missed his vault and I won. I was the freshman BOYS county pole vault champion. Thanks to my hard work and my coach who never gave up on me, my dream did come true! Hopefully other girls in Indiana will have the chance to pole vault in the near future as well.

What about you?
1. What is something you have dreamed of doing but never tried?

2. How could you go about finding out how to get involved in that thing?

_____

_____

_____

3. What are some obstacles that stand in the way of you doing that activity, and how can you creatively overcome them?

_____

_____

_____

Take Action!

Make a plan to get involved in something you've always wanted to try and set a goal for yourself. Tell someone that goal so he or she can remind you of it when you get discouraged.

Me, age 10, with my crazy, fun Aunt Tami

I SET GOALS

Most of the time I feel like a pizza at a sleepover — everyone wants a part of me — school, friends, family, church, boys, climbing, vaulting, volunteer work, me...There have been times in my life where I tried to give away more than I had, and I ended up sick or grouchy or not having anything left to give to the most important things. Now, I have been learning to give my energy to things in order of priority. I prioritize the demands on my time based on a long-term view of my life goals. I have come to realize that none of these demands is necessarily bad, it's just that I cannot be everything to everyone at all times.

The most important thing in my life is my faith. This is what gives me a framework for all my other decisions. My faith guides my moral development and is the source of my strength. I make sure to take time every day to learn more about being a Christian (the faith I have chosen) and to meditate on the teachings of my faith that are found in the Bible. I also meet weekly with other people who share my faith. They keep me on the right track as I navigate the other areas of my life by challenging me to ask myself questions about decisions I face.

After my faith, there is nothing more precious to me than my family — both immediate and extended. I try very hard to appreciate all my parents do to help me succeed. I especially appreciate my little brother. He is so generous, loving, and understanding. When I have an opportunity to visit my extended family, I rearrange things to make it happen. I never regret having those memories of chats with my aunt or math tutoring with my Nana.

School is something that gets a lot of my time and attention. It is the key to my future. Without an education, I would lose opportunities. I want to be a teacher, and I want to go out of state to college. I know that my grades need to be high to even have a chance of going to an out-of-state school. Plus, even if I loose my athletic ability, I will still have my brain.

Since I have a dream of going to the Olympics, the logical choice for the next most important thing is sports, especially pole vaulting and rock climbing. I often come home early from parties in order to be rested for a practice. I have also skipped ski trips and school functions to go to a meet or a competition. Now, remember, since school came before sports, then if I miss school for a sports event I do my school work before I go, not after.

You are probably thinking I am crazy because I have not even mentioned friends or boys but, you'll see, I am not as crazy as you think. How much study or practice time or energy have you wasted worrying about a friend or boy issue? Was it worth it? Well, I don't think so. I love my friends, but they know my priorities. When we are together, we have fun, but they cannot bring me peace like my faith or love me like my family or pave my future like my education or even fulfill a dream like my sports. They are just entertainment. As for boys, I have met some really nice guys, but I am not pushing it for now. I know it will be many years until I'll get married so I don't want to give away pieces of my heart over and over for the next eight years and then end up with nothing to give the man I marry. I try to choose my friends who are boys wisely.

Finally, I try to make wise decisions regarding my health just like I'd make good safety decisions. This is not a thing to prioritize, it is a fact of living. This translates into no drugs, no drinking, and no smoking for me. As for taking time out for myself, I take time for myself in all the above areas. I pray. I play games with my brother. I read. I swim and kickbox. I go to the mall. I talk on the phone. I try to live every moment of my life with a positive attitude and cheerful spirit. I also make sure my actions back up my words. If I say school is important but never do my homework, I am not believable. In the end, I even find that I have the time and energy to give back to my community a bit of what has been given to me by volunteering my time in various ways. I have a full, challenging, and happy life.

What about you?
1. List the things in your life that take up your time.

_____   _____

_____   _____

_____   _____

_____   _____

2. Now list them in order of priority and write why next to each.

_____   _____

_____   _____

_____   _____

Life Rocks!

3. Brainstorm ways you can volunteer in your community with the talents you have.

_____

_____

_____

Take Action!

Make a weekly schedule and look at how you spend your time. Adjust the schedule to reflect your priorities.

Me, age 12, and my friend Kally buried under part of my monkey collection (photo: Sports Illustrated/Heinz Kluetmeier)

I ENJOY A MESSY ROOM

I love my room. I am not really that private of a person but I do like having a space where I can make my own messes without having to clean them up immediately. If you were to come to my house, you would go upstairs to find my room. I am about to paint it, so it is plain white right now. I am going to paint it lavender, though, and attach vines all over the ceiling. On the vines I am going to hang many of my stuffed monkeys. My bed looks like it's made out of old crates. It is a rectangular box, with a mattress on top. There are poles at all four corners as well as around the top of the bed that hold up a pretend mosquito net. My comforter and pillows are made out of leopard prints of different colors and styles. I have bamboo shades on the windows and leopard bulletin boards on the wall. In addition to my bed, I have an old wooden desk and three bookshelves.

The thing that takes up 90 percent of the space in my room is my monkey collection. I have more than 350 monkeys of all shapes, sizes, uses, and styles. Over half of these are stuffed monkeys that I put on my bed, arrange in the corner, or will hang from the vines on my ceiling. I have dozens of monkey pictures, drawings, and calendars that fill my wall so full, it's like a collage. I have monkey lamps, monkey pens, monkey

91

tacks, and even monkey jewelry. My favorite monkey is Curious George because he reminds me of Georgie, my pet monkey.

The problem with having such an awesome collection of something like this is the time it takes to dust it. I have pretty bad allergies, and no one else in my family does. I am beginning to think it might have something to do with the dust that I harbor in the corners of my room. In my house, each person is in charge of cleaning his or her own room. There are no time limits on when this has to take place, although my mom has put safety limits on it. I think I am reaching health hazard levels at the moment. You know the dust is bad when you have to dust your mirror to find your face, or when you can blow on your desk and the dust creates a storm cloud in your room. I think I need to devote this whole weekend to ridding my room of dust.

My theory about a teenager's room is this. If you can live with it, and it is not a health or safety hazard, then the mess should not be noticed or commented on by other family members. Here is what I mean by "safety hazard:" just the other night, when my mom tried to tiptoe out of my room after rubbing my back, she tripped on my climbing bag and landed on her belly in a pile of monkeys and clean clothes. The next day I had to clear a path for her.

I also think teens should be able to paint, decorate, and otherwise be creative in their own room in any way they want. It's only temporary, and it's fun. One of my friends painted her room with chalkboard paint so now we can draw graffiti on it. Another girl I know glued random shoes on her ceiling and made footprints on the wall for decoration. It was very unique.

In the end, though, I am part of a family so I do my part to make things run smoothly around our house. I don't throw fits about cleaning and dusting my room (usually). I don't even try to pay my brother to do my chores. My chores are reasonable. I have to clean my room and bathroom each week.

I also have to either dust or vacuum the house each week and put away my laundry whenever I see that I have a pile of clothes in the laundry room. Each day, I have to pick up my clutter from around the house and dump it in my room. I can see the value in this sort of arrangement. No one has to do everything, but everything gets done. In all, my chores take an hour or two per week. I have to do them even if I am really busy so I learn to budget my time. Even though I enjoy a messy room, I also like to bring my friends over to a clean house.

What about you?
1. What do you like about your room?

_____

_____

_____

2. What is the most annoying thing about your room?

_____

_____

_____

Take Action!

Brainstorm ways to change or redecorate your room without using a lot of money. Look in magazines for crazy ideas for wall, curtains, and storage spaces. Start with something small like recovering a bulletin board or adding a glass top to a desk and putting a collage of photos under the glass, and then work on changing your room bit by bit.

Dad, Mom and me (age 14) between carpools and practices

I HAVE COOL PARENTS

Meet my mom and dad. They are not your typical parents. They were in college at Auburn University when I was born. They just fit me right into their college social life and never missed a step. Even when my brother was born two years later, they kept being active, silly, and adventurous. Now, they are in their late 30s and they are still young on the inside (and some people even think they look young on the outside.) My mom is a teacher, and my dad has degrees in religion, anthropology, and business. He owns two climbing gyms at the moment but who knows what he'll do after my brother and I are off to college? My parents really are the coolest parents in the world.

My mom is great because I can talk to her about anything. Sometimes I tell my friends what I tell my mom and they are shocked. I think it's important to get input from my mom who has already been a teenager once. She has good advice for me based on mistakes she made and things she learned. I never have to take her advice but it gives me something to think about. Mom is great with my friends because she will drop whatever she is doing to make her famous chocolate chip cookies for them at any time of the day or night. She also lets kids raid her fridge, so she makes sure to have plenty of teen-friendly food on hand. She never fusses about people spilling things on the carpet or loud noise at late hours. Plus, if someone is stranded and wants to hang out at our place, mom will always volunteer to go get her and to take her home.

My dad is really unique, too. He hangs out with my friends and gets to know their names. If they are involved in a sport he will go watch them play so he can talk to them about it. He also is crazy. Once he dug a hole in the yard so we could have a trampoline because mom said having it five feet off the ground was too dangerous. Another time, he talked mom into turning our guest room and hallway into a climbing room. If I need to just hang out without having to answer questions or tell about my day, I go to my dad. He is a good listener. He doesn't tell me I am wrong, he just lets me talk things out. When it comes to my sports, my dad is the ultimate supporter. Whenever I take up a new sport he buys a book on it so that he can know the rules and can feel like he is informed when he watches me. He is also very generous and will give me an opportunity even if it means that he has to give up something he would like to do.

Together, my parents are perfect. They get along great but they also do not hide their bad days from my brother and me. We get to see them work out their differences, and it helps us know what good communication is. My parents also check up on who I choose as friends. They know a lot of the teachers and coaches at my school as well as my youth pastor so they ask questions about the kids I hang out with. If they hear something that concerns them, they do not judge, they just make sure that I spend time with that person at our house so they can get to know that person better and watch for signs of trouble. Some kids think my parents are too involved. I think there is no such thing as too involved. I have friends I can trust, a good reputation, high morals, and good memories. If it were up to me to navigate these years alone, I think that I would not have the knowledge to keep all of those things in balance.

I am very close to my family. I really am not one of those people who you will hear complaining about her parents or her brother. I even love to visit my cousins, grandparents, and extended family. Sometimes I ask to make the five- or eight-hour drive to go see them. My brother is kind and unselfish. Even with all the opportunities I get, he never complains that it's not fair or demands something equal. He wants to be the president one day and I know he will succeed in that. I always tell him, my turn is now, but when we are older, I will be a teacher in a little town and you will be getting to travel and go to big events because you will be president. My parents taught me that family is where you find your strength and courage to go change the world. If that is true, the world better watch out for Clark and me.

What about you?
1. What do you appreciate about your parents?

_____

_____

_____

2. How have your parents helped you achieve your goals in your life?

_____

_____

_____

3. How are you similar to or different from your parents?

_____

_____

_____

Take Action!
  Write your parents a letter telling them that they are doing a good job raising you.

Me (age 13) hamming it up with Landen, Justin, Brent, and Zach before the Christmas dance

I WANT TO BE PROM QUEEN

The problem with being homeschooled was that I missed middle school. It's not the academics that were important, it was the lessons on how to be popular, cool, or just stay out of the way of those who were. I never learned how to form a group and keep others out of it. I never learned how to flirt with a boy by ignoring him and telling my friends to talk to him instead. I wasn't informed that only the popular people are allowed to sit in certain places and wear certain clothes. In fact, I didn't even know that it was so important to belong to the right group that I should change my hair, teeth, makeup, and attitude in order to have a better chance of getting picked to join one of the "in" groups. Instead, I entered ninth grade thinking everyone was my friend and everyone was in school to learn. Boy was I in for a shock!

Within a week of starting school I had settled into eating at a certain table at lunch, had identified the smartest people in most of my classes, and had said "Hi" to every teacher in the school at least once. I loved the whole school thing. I had to keep asking my locker neighbor to open my locker because it was either stuck or I had forgotten my combination. I packed my lunch every day, including a color change sprinkle yogurt. That yogurt entertained the others at my lunch table because they would all bet on the color it would turn to and keep track of who guessed it right the most. Yes, as you have guessed by now, I would have been classified as a nerd. But, since I did not yet know that people had labels other than freshman, sophomore, junior, and senior, I obliviously skipped through each day. By the end of the year, I came to the conclusion that I was a nerd, but I was a well-liked nerd so my friends and I decided we must be popular nerds. (Is that possible or have we upset the matrix by adding a new classification to the high school social system?)

As I became more and more aware of what it took to fit in I also became more and more stubborn about just being myself. I liked who I was (and still do), and I didn't want to give any of that up. I liked the Disney channel and didn't want to pretend I liked VH1 or BET just to be cool. My clothes were classy and cute, and I didn't want to have to buy them two sizes smaller and change the style just to get noticed by boys. When I was in class I actually had fun, and I didn't want to complain about my teachers and pretend that they were stupid just to fit in to the crowd. Every day after school I worked out for track and climbed for several hours. Many of the other girls spent hours on-line gossiping and plotting their next boy catch. I just couldn't see giving up my study time for that. So, I chose to remain a popular nerd rather than try to break into the popular crowds.

Even though I am a popular nerd, my climbing and vaulting successes have put me in the spotlight a bit. Whenever a girl succeeds, it is mandatory that other girls not in her group criticize her or make up rumors about her in order to bring her down and make themselves feel important again. Therefore, I became the topic of school gossip. If they weren't gossiping about my clothes from Target or my childish lunch box, then they were criticizing the people I hung around with and calling me snobbish. I quickly learned that there are some people you can never please or set straight. Knowing this doesn't make it any easier to hear bad things about yourself, or be totally ignored by some of your teammates on the girls' track team, but it does put things into perspective. Being me is the only person I can be, and I just make sure that my actions back up my words so people who take the time to get to know me will see that I am who I say I am. I am careful not to talk about other people or get involved in their lives. I just mind my own business and work hard at reaching my goals.

In the long run, I think the popular nerds will prevail. In high school, my grandmother says she was just like me. She was smart, athletic, and friendly but not part of the in crowd. She talked to everyone and did her own thing. Well, on prom night, all the people at her school who were not part of the most elite groups voted for her for prom queen. She said that when they announced that she had won, everyone was completely surprised, especially her. That just goes to show that I could still be prom queen. There is hope.

What about you?
1. How would you label your group of friends?

_____

_____

_____

2. What part of you do you hide or change when you are hanging out with your friends?

_____

_____

_____

3. If you could do it over, would you choose different friends or act differently around the friends you have now?

_____

_____

Life Rocks!

Take Action!

Choose a group of people outside your group of friends and get to know them this year. Sit with them at school sometimes, get their emails and IM names, invite them to do things with your group. See what happens to you and them after a year.

Me, age 14, signing autographs after speaking to a group of elementary school students

I VOLUNTEER

Living a life that makes a difference in the world is a core value of my family. My parents worked overseas in African villages training leaders, helping people learn to read, and teaching people how to manage their small businesses. I learned from their example that life is bigger than just the things I want. Over the years I have done a lot of volunteering. I have worked at The Children's Museum of Indianapolis as the mascot, Allie the Dinosaur, and in the International Gallery. I loved working with the kids. For over a year, I visited a widow once a week, taking her dinner to share and talking to her about her life and memories. She was so interesting. I have even helped the Red River Gorge Climber's Coalition have raffles and fundraisers at local competitions in order to raise money to keep climbing areas open to the general public. I also did an exhibition for them at their annual meeting. The areas where I love to climb are open to me due to their hard work. Currently, I am focusing my volunteer hours on climbing and fitness-related causes since my time is limited.

One thing that I do from time to time is go to a place called Jireh Sports. Jireh is a special place deep in the city of Indianapolis where kids can go and learn sports like wrestling and gymnastics as well as get tutoring for school, all for about a dollar a week. It is located in a large warehouse, and they have installed a climbing wall in it. When I go down there, I just hang out with the kids who come in to climb. I help them put on gear, show them ways to move on the wall that will help them get higher, and I encourage them as they climb. It is awesome to see the faces of girls, who thought they were too afraid to even try, when they get to the top. Often, the hardest part is getting them to put the gear away and go study. When I am not with them, I collect gently used gear from climbers I know and solicit new gear from companies to give to the center for the kids to use.

Several times per week I coach young girl climbers at my gym. Usually, I just set a time when they know I am going to be in and then anyone who wants to can come and climb with me. I play games with them that teach technique while still having fun. I challenge their weaknesses by helping them set goals. Most of all, I downplay competitiveness between them by building up the concept of encouraging each other and recognizing personal strengths. I spend more in-depth time with one particular girl named Autumn. I mentor her both in climbing and in life. I try to share with her the things I have learned and help her make good decisions about school, friends, boys, and life on and off the wall.

This year I have had the awesome opportunity of going to Washington, D.C. to lobby for various causes in Congress. One time I went to give a press conference about Title IX, which is a law that makes it illegal to discriminate against someone based on gender. This particularly applies to schools and sports. Since Title IX helped me get the right to pole vault as a girl in Indiana, I was able to speak to members of Congress about how important this law is to girls who are involved in sports. Another issue that I lobbied for was a program called PE 4 Life. I love this program because it's about making PE a class where kids learn how to be active and have fun doing it. It is different from traditional PE in that the focus is not on competitive and team sports. The focus is on teaching kids how to do many things, including rock climbing, that may be things they will choose as active hobbies when they are adults. Volunteering my time to try to make my voice heard on these issues was very satisfying. It was a way to impact future generations with good decisions. My experiences have even made me consider becoming a lawyer one day.

What about you?

1. What have you done for someone else this week?

_____

_____

_____

2. Brainstorm some ways to volunteer in your community

_____

_____

_____

Take Action!

I want to challenge you to find something that you can do with your time that can make someone else smile or make a difference in some way. Start small by volunteering to watch the little girls next door for an hour while their mom goes to the store without them. You could write encouraging notes to people who are having bad days. You could even go to a nursing home and play games with people there for an hour each week. The idea is to do something. Focus on someone besides yourself and your friends for a small portion of each week. At the end of this book is a project called THE HAPPY BOX that I do. It is very easy to do and I encourage you to try it. It will make a difference in someone's day. When you do take this challenge, write me a note and tell me about your project. I love hearing how kids are changing the world. It makes me hopeful about the future of our world.

Studying hard with my friend Sebastian.
I like to study with friends

I THINK SCHOOL IS GREAT

As you know, I was homeschooled all my life until I was 13 years old and started ninth grade. At that point, my parents and I decided that it was a good time to go to school so that I could begin participating in school-sponsored events like sports and theatre. My parents wanted the perfect academic situation for me so they looked around the city at many private and public high schools. After a year long search, we decided that Lawrence Central was the best place for me. The problem was that it was out of our school district so we had to pay out-of-district tuition until we could sell our house and move. We chose Lawrence Central because of its diversity, its emphasis on character education, its size, and its athletic offerings, particularly in pole vault.

My freshman year was unforgettable. I had my first crush on someone who didn't even know I existed. I took my first bubble tests, and I studied for my first final exams. I even rode a yellow school bus for the first time ever. The best part of public school was sitting in a class of over 30 students discussing ideas together. The hardest part was all the writing assignments and projects for my English/World Cultures class. Also, when I realized how many students cheated on tests and copied homework instead of doing it themselves, I was confused. Why would students who studied or did the work themselves want to give it away? Why would someone want to take the chance of getting caught cheating? As the year went on, I realized that people have many views of education. In order for me to reach my life goals, I knew I had to be careful to stay focused on my goals because there were many people and situations out there that could pull me off course. I ended the year exhausted and ready to be a sophomore.

This year has been different. It is easier to know what teachers expect since I have a year of experience behind me. I only forgot my athletic locker combination for a few weeks, and I never forgot my hall locker combination. I finally felt comfortable contributing to discussions in class and asking teachers questions about their subjects. I have learned how to stand up for my rights when I feel a teacher may not be being fair, and I have learned the appropriate way to stand up to my peers as well. The most challenging part of this year has been my drama class. I have a tough time memorizing plus I don't think I was meant to be on stage, so it is a lot of work for me. I thought Drama would be an easy A, so I also realized that learning is hard work, no matter what the subject is.

Sometimes it is particularly hard for me to get all my work done and learn all I need to know because I travel a lot. I travel to climbing competitions all over the USA and the world. I also travel to pole vault competitions around the USA. In addition to that, I am out of school when I speak to other schools, make appearances on talk shows, have photo shoots, and do things like lobby in Washington, D.C. All of these are awesome opportunities but they do mean missing school. I try to get my assignments before I leave town and do them while I am gone. This way, when I return I am already caught up. That means that I spend a lot of time in airports and hotels reading and studying. Sometimes I take a laptop computer to communicate with my teachers for clarification or talk to my classmates about assignments. Every once in awhile, I drive to Nashville, Tennessee, to see my grandmother, who is a math tutor. She reviews my geometry with me and teaches me things that are coming up so that I have a jump start on the class. Math is the only subject that is hard to teach to yourself — especially geometry!

So, why do I love school? I have made a decision to love it on purpose. I realize that education is the road to the future. Without college, I cannot be a teacher, a spy, or a lawyer. The teachers at my school are my partners in my journey, so I try to appreciate them when they help me. If I am confused, I ask questions. I never sleep in class. I respect deadlines. I always do my homework. Whenever there is extra credit, I do it. Even if I am not currently in a certain teacher's class, I still speak to that teacher in the hallway. I try to follow the rules of the school and have a good attitude toward learning. Character goes a long way in education. If teachers know you respect them and you really want to learn, they will be thrilled to teach you. I know this from experience.

What about you?

1. What are your goals in life?

_____

_____

_____

_____

2. How is education going to help you reach those goals?

_____

_____

_____

_____

3. How do you show your teachers that you want to learn?

_____

_____

_____

Life Rocks!

Take Action!

Think of four colleges that interest you. Even if you are young, it doesn't hurt to dream. Look these colleges up on the Internet. Make a poster for your room that tells about each college. Make sure to find out what grades they require for you to get accepted and what subjects you need to take in high school. As you get closer to college, make sure you are exceeding these expectations so you will be certain to be accepted.

Me (age 14) with some of my friends from the boys' track team after winning the conference championship

I MAKE TIME FOR FRIENDS

Choosing good friends is one of the hardest tasks in life. It is hard for me to find friends who are loyal and who like me for being Tori and not because it is cool to know "the climber girl." In my life, it is also important to find friends who are confident enough with their own lives that they are not jealous of mine. I like people who are active and spontaneous. The friendships that last with me are with people who do not have to spend all their time with me. They have their own lives outside of our friendship. When I look at the people who are my closest friends I cannot see a pattern. They are all very different. They are diverse in many ways including their personalities, lifestyles, and their life goals. Let me introduce you to a few.

Kally, Jessica, JoAnna, and Danielle (Dany) are my four best friends who are girls. They do not even know each other. Danielle was a competitor against me when I was a skater. I used to write her good luck notes before competitions and that is how we became friends. She lives an hour away from me so we get together on school breaks. Kally lived behind my old house and used to play on my trampoline with me. She is a swimmer who is not afraid to tell me that I am being selfish. She is good for me. Jessica had a locker next to mine the first day of ninth grade. She is a Christian like me, and she helps me keep my priorities straight because she is so focused on hers. JoAnna and I were born the same summer in Auburn, Alabama. We have been buddies since then. I love JoAnna because she really knows all the parts of the real Tori and just accepts me how I am. She lives in Atlanta.

A lot of my other friends are guys. Many of those guys are on the track team with me. When I was 12 years old I started working out with the high school track team so I instantly had 80 big brothers. Over the past few years, I have built deep friendships with several of these guys. They are really good to have around when I need advice about relationships from a guy's perspective and when I need to vent about my athletic frustrations. They push me to work hard at practice and encourage me to be stronger and faster. I appreciate having these guys as friends because it shows me what it feels like to be appreciated as an athlete. Without guy friends, my life would be very shallow.

Since I travel a lot, I have actually made good friends in my sport and in other extreme sports. These friends live in places like North Carolina, California, and Canada but we have deep friendships because we share a bond. Our bond is our unusual talent and our young age in the adult world of our sport. When we are all at an event where the adults are gong to parties and staying out late, we spend time talking in hotel lobbies, swimming, watching movies, and teaching each other our sports. Pat, one of my closest friends in this category, is fun to talk to because he understands what it is like to be a normal high schooler by day and a superstar climber (kayaker for him) by night. When I am around these friends I am truly myself. I don't worry about being popular, worry about them being jealous, or even worry that someone will start rumors. These friends accept me as a climber and a kid. They don't care what I wore to school last week or who I ate lunch with. Our time together is relaxing. I don't see these friends much so when I do get time with them, we end up staying up to wee hours catching up on each other's lives and just enjoying being "normal" extreme teens.

Making time for my friends is tricky. When I have not seen one of my friends in awhile, I call or send an email to catch up. Since I am out of town a lot, I let my friends know that I am thinking of them by picking up trinkets for them on my travels. I wrap my gifts in barf bags from airplanes. When I have a break coming up, I plan ahead so that I do not get so busy that I have no extra time to visit my friends who live far away. Now, after years of juggling my travels, my studies, my sports, and my friends, arranging my life to make time for friends is a habit. Friends are the people who keep me sane when my life is crazy. I appreciate my friends.

What about you?

1. List your friends.

_____   _____

_____   _____

_____   _____

_____   _____

_____   _____

_____   _____

2. Next to each write how you met and why you have stayed friends.

Life Rocks!

Take Action!

Give each of your friends a picture of you with a note on the back saying thank you for being your friend.

These are my African friends. They love the Happy Box.

THE HAPPY BOX

Take a big box and decorate it in happy colors. Cut a hole in the top about five inches square. Put a smile on the side of the box and label it *The Happy Box*.

Put the box in churches, schools, family businesses, or other public places (make sure to get permission first!). Make a sign asking people to donate "happy meal" type toys. Basically, the toys should be small and pre-packaged. Collect until the box is full. Then seal the box and mail it to needy children overseas. Make sure to include the complete and correct address. This box will put a happy face on children around the world.

I got this idea from my time in Africa. I remember how the village children would come over and play with my toys. They would want to take my things home and keep playing because they had no toys. Often when my grandma would send me things that were small, I would give them to my friends to take home. I knew they would get more out of them and I could live without them.

When I came to the USA, I started saving my kids meal toys to send over. Then I started saving my allowance and baby sitting money for postage. I made a box, named it, and put it in my church. In two weeks, it was full so I sent the first box over in time for Christmas. The project is growing. These toys can be sent anywhere — to kids in Israel or Africa or Afghanistan. This is something anyone can do to put a happy face on children anywhere.

Mom, Dad, Nana, Grandpa, Clark and me (age 9)

THANK YOU!

First of all, I want all of you to know that profits from this book are going toward a fund to help build proper houses for my friends in Benin.

Next, I have so many people to thank. No one is an island, and I am who I am today because of the wonderful people in my life now and over the past 14 years. I am the richest person in the world because of these people.

So here it goes. Mom, Dad, and Clark — you are the best family in history. I have a lot to live up to as a parent one day. I hope you'll help me. I'll visit you in the White House, Clark! Nana, Grandpa, Nancy, David, Carol, Little Dave — thanks for letting my parents raise me in their own crazy way. Don't worry, it's working out fine. Thanks also for loving me so much. Cookie Grandpa, Tami, Tom, Greta, Leona — thanks for being my wild side of the family. Your adventures make me never want to stop living life for fun. To my cousins, aunts, uncles, and grandma (the Eggers Clan) in Iowa — thanks for being so supportive of your town girl cousin. I'll never stop coming home to see you — EVER!

"Uncle" Doug, "Aunt" Robyn, Andrea (my first editor) and Nicole — thanks for being like family to me and cheering for me in all I do. To my CMF family and my mission family in

117

Benin — thanks for filling in for my aunts and uncles who were in America. You will relate to the experiences of this book more than anyone.

Kati, my life mentor — you have been guiding me and listening to me since I was 11. I know you'll still be there when I am 111! Thank you!

All my coaches over the years — Pete, figure skating — you were to first to believe in me as an athlete, and I'll never forget you. Dad, soccer — sorry, I know you thought I had potential. Thanks for not pushing. Frank, Katie, Obe, climbing — Each of you pushed me and challenged me in new ways. I am a better climber and coach because of your input. Coach Holman and Tim Richey, pole vault — you two let me be a little girl with a big dream and you never let on if you had your doubts about me. And the Lawrence Central boys track team — thanks for letting a little girl practice with you without mocking her or making her miserable. You guys are true gentlemen!

My school, Lawrence Central High School — thanks for finding a way to let me pass PE so I can graduate instead of having to homeschool and for recognizing that I can be Tori, the super star, and still learn all that I need to learn in high school even if I have to miss 30 days doing it. And to all the teachers there who care enough to come in every day ready to teach something to all us alien teenagers. I appreciate you.

And last of all, my friends. Sorry if I leave someone out. You know it's an accident if I do. You guys have seen my good and horrible sides, my sick and healthy days, my wise and poor decisions, my childish and mature moments… and you are still there. You are the greatest! Too bad you live all over the world. The families who have supported me are: the Collins, the Sellers, the Dukes, the Huffmans, the Richardsons, the Rubins. My Peace Corps buddies are: Jennifer, Kristen, Valerie, Joanne, Lisa, Andrew, Dan, and Rachel, and all the others from the Benin years. My far-flung friends are Kerri S., Katherine V., Arienna G., Zoe R., Joanna C., Pat K., Jeremy P.,

Kenny, Dany. And my high school buddies are: Kally R., Jessica, Alexis, Jamie; my lunch buddies, Brad, Tyler, Sebastian, Mike, Khayri, Danny, Ben, Casey, Ann, Charisse, Erica, Naiasha, Britney, and Misha. Thanks for being friends with this popular nerd.

I owe everything to my creator and savior, Jesus Christ. He gave me all these people and a talent to boot. I dedicate my life to Him.

Look These Up!

1. **www.usclimbing.org** — information on competitive rock climbing for youth and adults

2. **www.usatf.org** — information on track and field, especially youth competitions

3. **www.toriallen.com** — this one tells you more about me. There are even videos of me climbing!

4. **www.pe4life.org** — tells all about new ideas to make PE a lifelong activity starting in kindergarten!

5. **www.womensportsfoundation.org** — a great Web site about women in sports, including young girls

6. **www.galyans.com** — find a store near you and go try out their climbing wall for FREE! That's how I got started.

7. **www.cmfi.org** — look here for ideas on where to send your happy boxes

8. **www.climbtimeindy.com** — this is my climbing gym. Come climb with me!